NOT OUR
DAY TO DIE

NOT OUR DAY TO DIE

Testimony from the Guatemalan Jungle

Michael Sullivan

Terra Nova Books

Santa Fe, New Mexico

Library of Congress Control Number 2017942519

Distributed by SCB Distributors, (800) 729-6423

Terra Nova Books

Published by Terra Nova Books, Santa Fe, New Mexico.
www.TerraNovaBooks.com
ISBN 978-1-938288-90-6

For Martina

Contents

Foreword

This is a book that grabbed me from the outset. Perhaps it captivated me because I lived part of that history years after Mike, the anthropologist/pilot, perhaps because of the testimonies themselves: vibrant, concrete, humane, not overstated, never exaggerated—hence, one trusts them. They are filled with psychological irony and observations, and in some parts are poetic.

I can attest that we are hearing a group of great storytellers. Maybe this is because from the beginning of the repression and the massacres, the people of Ixcán did not have to remain silent, as happened in most Guatemalan towns. No, they talked and talked, and created a memorial that may rise a couple of inches above reality, but that is what gives storytelling its breath.

For people who still doubt what we have said about the massacres in Guatemala's jungle, this book is a testimonial to the terrible things that took place; its authenticity is irrefutable. The massacre of Cuarto Pueblo appears in one place or another in various testimonies. In addition to what I already knew, other things still come to light for me. For example, I didn't know that because of a car malfunction, José Sales escaped the burning of the Spanish Embassy on January 31, 1980. There are other incredible things, fit for a movie, that I didn't know either, like the story of the girl pursued by a helicopter in a jungle clearing while carrying her little brother on her back, or about the man bitten by a snake through his boot. There are many such incidents.

These stories all take place within the framework of an oral history. It is not just autobiography but collective history: the oppressive work conditions on the southern coast; the journey from the highlands to colonize the jungle amid the sufferings of poverty but also the wonder at the fertility of the place; and later on, the guerrillas and the massacres by the army; the fleeing to exile in Mexico or the resistance, living and hiding in the jungle; then the return from Mexico or the emergence from the jungle; and now, a more-scattered life that many compare with a sort of lost paradise of the co-operative's first days, or as someone else talks of, a new stage: migration to the U.S.

At the core of this story is always Father Guillermo Woods, whom they credit for the land they enjoy in the Ixcán, and refer to with emotion and respect—"Padre Guillermo, may he rest in peace." There, in his circle of companions, is Miguel—or Mike or Miko— the pilot who flew out the sick and the cargoes of cardamom when Woods, also a pilot, couldn't do it all himself. There is continual gratitude to the Catholic Church for its help to the refugees and members of the resistance. Like beautiful clouds on a bright day that accompany the storytellers—men and women—is the reference to dreams, in the form of mysterious warnings that became reality and bear witness to the deep indigenous culture of most of the storytellers, and maybe also to the culture of liminality in which they lived, neither here nor there, where the subconscious seems to slip through while one is asleep. Tied closely to the dreams is the grateful interpretation of God as the savior from so many dangers. This is about a deeply religious people who are not fixated on why God let so many die in the massacres but thank him because they are alive.

There are distinct perspectives among the people's voices. Not only are there differences in age, the year of arrival in the jungle, whether they knew Padre Guillermo personally or through third parties, and gender (women and men speaking almost in the same proportion). There are also differences in perspective according to what the person experienced, for example thirteen years as a refugee versus not having gone even for one month to Mexico and saying with exultation: "all the time I was in the resistance." Another different perspective is that of the people now in the Ixcán and those who went on to live in other places, such as Petén, Escuintla, Jacaltenango and probably lost the right to a parcel of land in the jungle, although they are left with a thread of memory that ties them back to the Ixcán.

Finally, although it might appear subtler, there is the perspective of the people who remained in the lands of the co-ops, like May-alán, and those who went to form a new settlement in Primavera del Ixcán, by the Chixoy River. There is one testimony of a man who was living in army-controlled territory. Along with others, he walked to his farm in territory defended by the guerrillas. The guerrillas shot him.

Sadly, war put siblings against each other. He had previously hosted me in a refugee camp.

My thanks to Michael Sullivan for this captivating book. I believe that memory, even if it rises three or four inches above the earth and starts wearing an aura of myth, can give the people strength to face the future. If not, let's take a look at how the story of the Gospels, raised maybe more than four inches, has given an identity to a whole movement throughout centuries without losing their foundation in history. This is what makes these accounts so compelling; they are not mere myth. The mythical impetus, innate in the telling of stories, even in the most accurate and objective autobiography, contributes to the narrative a force of creativity and significance. History points to the terrible, unanswerable, and irrefutable fact of the massacres, but the people speak not only of the massacres but also that "we are alive," and thus, it is good news.

—Ricardo Falla, S.J., Author of *Quiche Rebelde; Masacres de la Selva, Ixcán, Guatemala;* and *Historia de un Gran Amor*

Preface

In 1972, I departed the United States for Latin America, looking for flying work. By chance, in Guatemala City, I met Father Bill Woods (known as Padre Guillermo or Padre Woods to the people he served). He hired me, but when it soon became clear he couldn't afford to pay me, I became a volunteer instead—which I remained for the next two and a half years. It was my first connection with the Ixcán, an area of jungle lowland that was essentially uninhabited but slowly became "homesteaded" by about twenty-five hundred families over the years. My "job" was flying a plane between all the jungle airstrips and the provincial capitals of Huehuetenango and Quiche.

The planes carried people moving out to settle as well as supplies for the co-op stores, medicine, animals (everything you can think of except a horse). We took health aides to the Maryknoll Sisters' hospital in Jacaltenango for training, and flew out any medical emergencies. The co-ops purchased corn, beans, and cardamom to give the people a commercial outlet for their crops. Taking these from Ixcán to sell in Huehuetenango kept the planes filled in an attempt to help pay for the service. The price for the thirty-to-forty-minute trip for both passengers and freight was $3 for a hundred pounds.

Under the principal cooperative of Ixcán Grande were "local" co-ops in each town with an airstrip: Mayalan, Xalbal, Pueblo Nuevo (also called La Resureccion), Cuarto Pueblo, and Los Angeles. The area served by each of these local co-ops was divided into centers. Some centers went by their number, such as the First Center

(Primer Centro); others were given names by Padre Eduardo Doheney, the Maryknoll priest who started the project in the Ixcán, or
by the people themselves.

The Ixcán this book describes was an area bounded on the west
by the Rio Ixcán, on the east by the Rio Xalbal, on the north by the
Mexican border, and on the south by a generally east-west line about
eight to ten miles south of Mexico. In the 1970s, it was very peaceful. I flew out several people with machete wounds, but they had
occurred in "ordinary" activities, not fights. No one was ever killed
that I heard of. On a national scale, the revolutionary movement
was in a rebuilding and regrouping stage after its leader and many
others were killed in the late 1960s.

In those years, I met many of the people who have been interviewed for this book. When I first arrived, I lived by myself in the
First Center. Dominga Pablo Lucas would prepare dinner for me
and send it over with Maria Matias, her daughter. Maria was a child,
and probably terrified of the strange foreigner living next door. She
would hand me the food and be gone like a shot.

Mariano Martín Pablo worked in the co-op store at Mayalan in
the 1970s and was with me in 1993 as part of the first group from
Mexico in the "organized return" negotiated by the refugees and
the Guatemalan government. José Diaz Perez and his wife, Luciana
Rojas Diaz, were in Mayalan on the night a huge windstorm destroyed many houses. Chus Camposeco walked for a day with me
and Bob Coe, a volunteer carpenter from Houston, when we went
to work on building the next airstrip in Pueblo Nuevo. And Juan
Silvestre Quinones played the marimba I often fell asleep listening
to at night in Mayalan.

Chepe Sales was tending the store/clinic in Xalbal. Later at a
camp in Mexico, he told me that he felt the violence between the
army and the guerrillas and *campesinos* (peasant farmers) was so bad
in Ixcán because the people there had become independent from
the old migrant worker system, which he felt posed an economic
threat to the status quo of the big landowners. He was one of the
negotiators representing the refugees in talks with the U.N. and the

Guatemalan government regarding a return from Mexico. He is amazingly astute politically, and shared many stories about emergencies and close scrapes he shared with Bill Woods.

Although the runway in Pueblo Nuevo was operational, it was very marginal, with high terrain at both ends. There was no town yet, no houses, just the clinic run by Gonzalo Ross. I got to know Gonzalo because he was always glad for company in the short time my plane was on the ground.

When I returned to the U.S. in the fall of 1975 to go to school, the army was just beginning to make its presence felt in Ixcán. The following year, when I returned briefly after an earthquake to help with airlifts and medical supplies, I noticed an increased military presence and growing uneasiness among the people.

Around 1988, I walked through the Ixcán to place a grave marker on the spot in the First Center where one of our pilots, Jon Stork, was buried, and I returned the next year to work on a documentary about the war. Xalbal was still in existence but now was occupied by ex-soldiers. In Mayalan, there was a similar fort and a couple of civilian families, one of them the family of Valentin Juan Domingo. On a later trip, I walked with a film crew to Pueblo Nuevo where there was an army fort. It didn't amount to much, just a sandbag perimeter with tents and trenches inside. It was a bit surreal, with tall green grass growing everywhere. But also everywhere were burnt posts thrusting upward. They were all that remained of the town.

Teresa de Jesus I met when she was a refugee in Mexico. She was a member of Mama Maquin, an organization of refugee women set up to help widows and orphans. Maria Matias, the child who would leave my dinner and run, eventually became the national chairwoman of Mama Maquin.

In December 1995, I returned to the Ixcán and flew for a year as the co-op towns were being repopulated. The war had wound down. There were occasional firefights at a fort about three miles away from Mayalan where we lived. But out there, three miles was a long way, and there was no immediate danger. Word of the cease-fire eventually made it to the jungle.

I had funding to fly for a year. My plane was too small to be of great practical use, but it was a huge psychological boost to the people. I flew passengers, freight, and—most important—could transport the sick.

At one point, a forensics team requested flights from Guatemala City to Cuarto Pueblo to return the bones taken from a mass grave. I knew that over three hundred people had died in the massacre there, and was concerned about how many flights would be needed—but in a moment that still haunts me, I saw that it could all be done in one trip. There was six hundred pounds of bone fragments, nothing more. The whole town waited in Cuarto, and the remains were taken to a mausoleum the people had built at the cemetery.

By the early 2000s, passable roads had been built into the area of the Ixcán, and the need for small planes diminished. I still return when I can, especially trying to make the trip in November for the anniversary of Bill Woods' death.

Acknowledgments

It takes a village to raise a child . . . and perhaps several villages to write a book. First of all was the incredible amount of trust, openness, and honesty shown by the people of Ixcan, those interviewed and their families. This has been from the beginning a volunteer affair—friends editing, commenting, correcting. Several from the immigrant community in the states helped with agrarian vocabulary that was not to be found in any dictionary. My thanks to you all.

In no particular order are some of those who have helped me in many and various ways:

Dave La Buda
Mirna Castellanos de Hollstegge
Chico Miron
Itzel, y la Familia Nieves
Arianna Sullivan
Martina Sullivan
Jennifer Hollstegge de Archila
Aimeé Castro de Flores
Rob and Jennifer Rice
Los de Agua del Pueblo
Rolando Lopez
David Hollstegge
Flor de Maria Oliva
Jeanie Sullivan

Aimée Hollstegge
Robert Dailey
Bill Woods
Jane Birk
Juanita Montoya
Bayita O'Rourke
Kieran Sullivan
Brian O'Rourke
Mike Perkins
Shayla Blatchford
Adam Horowitz
John Woods
Margarita Floricelda Ross
Miguel TePaz

A Word About a Name

The word Ixcán comes from the Kanjobales. In Kanjobal, the name is not Ixcán but "Yichcan," meaning the end of the highlands. In the old days, our fathers, looking out over the great jungle from Santa Eulalia, said that the sky and the land ended here: "Yichcan" or "Ichk'an." Yichcan has the significance that the sky falls [to meet] the earth, the end of the *alto,* the highlands. That is what they thought. It was the edge of the earth. So they named it Ichk'an.

—Juan Juarez Juan

Introduction

In the 1950s in Guatemala, 2.2 percent of the people owned 70 percent of the land, but only about 12 percent was actively farmed. The United Fruit Company owned about 42 percent of the arable land. Most of the population lived mainly by agriculture, but few had enough land to support themselves. Men and boys especially were present in their villages for planting and harvest seasons but spent the rest of the year working on the large cotton, sugar, and coffee *fincas* (estates). This largely indigenous rural population lived for the most part in abject poverty.

In 1952, President Jacobo Árbenz Guzmán started nationalizing unused land to redistribute to the poor. He paid the United Fruit Company the value it had declared its land to be worth for tax purposes. But United Fruit, which actually considered the land much more valuable than that, had two very powerful friends in the U.S.— the Dulles brothers, whose law firms had represented the company. Allen Dulles was director of the CIA, and John Foster Dulles the U.S. secretary of state. In 1954 under the Eisenhower administration, the U.S. engineered a coup overthrowing Árbenz and installing a former army colonel, Carlos Castillo Armas, in his place. The conservative hierarchy of the Catholic church supported the change, and hence was given a free hand by the new regime. Ironically, this led to the more liberal Maryknoll Fathers and Brothers, and later the Maryknoll Sisters, being invited into the country.

In 1965, Padre Eduardo inaugurated a land reform project in the uninhabited jungle lowland area known as the Ixcán. The land was what was termed "baldio," uncultivated and not used or owned by anyone. The Cooperative Ixcán Grande, which the government was willing to let have it, laid out "centers" in the style of Israeli kibbutzes and pie-shaped parcels of land radiating out from them. The first center—referred to as Centro Uno, or Primer Centro—remained the entry point for nearly all future members of the co-ops.

Padre Woods took over in 1969 and, working with David Hollstegge, expanded the co-op greatly until about twenty-five hundred families had received a *parcela*, a farm. For ease of surveying, the lines were now run out as squares or rectangles. Five co-operatives were formed under the umbrella of the Cooperativa Ixcán Grande.

David trained people from the co-ops as surveyors. Lines were run to lay out the parcelas, and in the process, relatively flat spots were sought to build landing strips and locate the towns nearby. There were no roads into the area. To get there, one took a bus ten to fourteen hours from Huehuetenango to Barillas, then rode in the back of a pickup for four hours, then walked for one to three days.

After the original settlements, those who wished to join the co-ops had to live for six months with a *padrino*, literally a god-father but in this case more of a sponsor. Then the community voted on whether to accept the newcomer. Those who were approved could select a parcela through a lottery system. On the day parcelas were given out, numbers were put in a hat, then the people drew a number and picked their farm in order of the numbers drawn.

The parcelas were quite large for the time and place: twenty-eight acres. Those settling there were given five years to pay for the land. (Average income at the time was about a hundred seventy quetzales a year, equivalent to $170 U.S.) Getting titles to the land took years, but they were finally granted in 1976 in the name of the Cooperativa Ixcán Grande as the owner. The idea was that this would protect the campesinos from losing their land through debt, fraud, etc. It was a system that remained in effect until 1996, when the titles were converted to allow individual ownership.

A big part of the cooperative program involved education in many areas. Health aides worked with the people, as they were being further trained themselves. Schools were built and staffed, and literacy programs were begun for adults. Clinics and general stores opened in each town with an airstrip, which was built by communal labor. People were brought in to train the members in how a co-op functioned. Agricultural consultants introduced new vegetables and other crops. All the programs together promoted what is called in Spanish *conciencitizacion,* roughly "consciousness raising."

November 1960 had seen the beginning of the revolutionary movement in Guatemala when a group of young army officers led by Marco Antonio (Yon) Sosa attempted a coup. The fighting went on for some time, mostly in the eastern part of the country. (Ixcán at the time was virtually unoccupied.) With advisers from the American Green Berets, the CIA, and the U.S. Army Eighth Special Forces Group, the insurgency was essentially defeated by 1970. The social inequalities that had led to the movement remained, however, and the revolution went underground as it built broader-based support.

In the mid '70s, Ixcán was a sort of utopian island in the midst of Guatemalan life. There was no army presence and no police presence—neither organization being exactly representative of "law and order."

After the big earthquake in 1976, a visit to the Ixcán made clear the palpable uneasiness among the people in the co-ops. The fear grew along with an increase in control, and eventually outright repression by the army. The leadership of the co-ops was selectively targeted for disappearance, a noun that became a verb, to be "disappeared." Later, the army progressed to outright assassination of co-op directors, schoolteachers, catechists, and then of anyone suspected of being one of or assisting the guerrillas.

On January 31, 1980, a group of displaced peasant farmers occupied the Spanish embassy in Guatemala City to protest kidnappings and murders by elements of the Guatemalan Army. Over the protests of the Spanish ambassador, police attacked the building with incendiary explosives, and then kept those in the burning embassy from leaving; thirty-six people were killed. The funeral of the victims attracted hundreds of thousands of mourners. Some of the organizers of the occupation had been from Ixcán.

In the Ixcán itself, violence increased exponentially. The Guerrilla Army of the Poor (EGP) attacked the army fort at Cuarto Pueblo, and for a time, the army withdrew from the Ixcán. Rejoicing, the people burned down the forts. But the army returned in force. A scorched-earth policy followed. Everything was a target: animals killed, crops burned, fruit trees uprooted, towns burned, and villages massacred. The worst massacre, in Cuarto Pueblo, took place over several days in March 1982. There are some reports that the army said the massacre was in response to the earlier guerrilla attack on the fort.

Throughout the Ixcán, those who survived fled. Some returned to their original mountain villages, others crossed the Ixcán border into Mexico, and a third group of men, women, and children survived for sixteen years hiding in the jungle. These people were called the Comunidades de Poblacion en Resistencia (CPR), Communities of the People in Resistance. Those in Mexico were originally near the border, in Chiapas. But because of incursions of the Guatemalan army and Mexico's own fear of destabilization in its most neglected area, the refugees were moved to a series of camps farther away. The United Nations High Commission for Refugees was instrumental in setting up the camps, and later in helping with the logistics of the return to Guatemala.

Jungle took over the co-op towns as the war raged on, encompassing the whole nation. There were repeated army sweeps through the Ixcán, reminiscent of U.S. "Search and Destroy" operations in Vietnam. In the Ixcán, the army was eventually reduced to living in forts in a state of siege. In the fort at Cuarto Pueblo, it had trouble at least for a time resupplying even enough food for the garrison. But the guerrilla movement was never strong enough to overrun the forts, and for most of the conflict could not protect the general population from the army.

Some people were repatriated from Mexico back to Ixcán during the war years, but they were exploited and forced to live just outside the forts as a sort of human shield for the army. Some stayed, but many soon moved elsewhere.

The first organized return of refugees from Mexico took place in January 1993, organized by the Permanent Committee of Guatemalan Refugees together with the U.N High Commission for Refugees. The journey took over a year for many. The original group stopped at a place called Victoria 20 Enero (for the date they crossed into Guatemala on their return, the twentieth of January). Others essentially camped at a crossroads called Veracruz for a year, pressuring the army to leave the Ixcán area as promised in the return agreements signed between the government and those who had fled to Mexico. Later, a cease-fire with the guerrillas was agreed to, and peace accords were signed in 1996.

Many of the parcelas around Xalbal had been given by the army to ex-soldiers and other supporters, and these were never recovered by the co-op. Most other co-op members who returned got their own land back, and some received the land of those who had been killed or decided not to return.

A considerable group of those who had been in the CPR communities—including former co-op members and others from the surrounding areas—stayed together and now live in a "nearby" community called Primavera. ("Nearby" in 1996 meant fifteen minutes by plane and then three hours by canoe. In 2010, the trip from Mayalan to Primavera could be made in about six or seven hours by jeep.)

The lands of Ixcán Grande are once again full of people. The cooperatives are less of a factor than before but exist on a smaller scale. Sixteen years were lost, along with countless lives.

The story of those years—of how the people of the Ixcán survived, and of the many who didn't—was one that had to be told. I returned there in 2010 and twice in 2011 to do the interviews that form this book. The people I talked with were ones I had known from the '70s, and the late '90s when I flew there again. I went to their houses with a little recorder and asked if they remembered the early days of the Cooperativa Ixcán Grande, of their first coming down to the Ixcán, and what their life had been like in the years of repression. This is what they told me:

The
Interviews

Alejandro Ramirez Cruz
Primavera, June 1, 2010

I am from Tierra Fria, the highlands—from Todos Santos, Huehuetenango. My mother had a tiny piece of land there in Todos Santos that was just big enough for the house, so I didn't stay there. I was on the south coast working in a place called La Maquina. I had to borrow a plot of land to plant corn so that we would have something to eat. I worked there for eight years, planting a little corn, earning a little, just enough to stay alive and not

Alejandro Ramirez Cruz

die of hunger. Then the rent for the land went up; there were too many people and not enough land.

Padre Eduardo put out a notice that there was land in Ixcán Grande, and I came in 1974. We arrived in Primer Centro in May. We were given a place to stay with a *parcelista* in Mayalan.

Usually when a person arrived, he was on probation for six months to see if he really needed land. The directors of the co-op took into account whether the person did community work, if they drank, if they got along with the others. If they were a "good" person, they were given a parcela of four hundred *cuerdas*, (about twenty-eight acres), a lot in town, and a place in the market. The person then was a member of the co-operative.

The parcela I was given was in Pueblo Nuevo, which was the third of five co-operatives. The first was Mayalan, then Xalbal, then Pueblo Nuevo. After us there was Cuarto Pueblo and Los Angeles. More people came later but didn't get land.

It was the first time I'd had a piece of land. My father and mother came, and we began to work. We built the airstrip of Pueblo Nuevo with voluntary communal work. It was a lot of work to fix up. We also worked on paths and *brechas* (paths cut through the jungle, often for survey lines). We complied with the rules of the co-operative out of love for the land. We needed it for the family; we had two children. We worked, planting coffee, cardamom, and corn. We had animals: pigs, chickens, ducks, dogs—good hunting dogs. We hunted armadillo and *tepezcuintle* (paca).

I remember Bill and David, the engineer, very well. David, Bill, someone else called Tonino. Those people helped us . . . . I don't know if David and Tonino are alive. Padre Bill was assassinated. He was for the poor. He blessed our lives. He shed his blood for us—the indigenous and the poor. He gave us a piece of land, and we improved our lives. The good thing is we haven't lost the seeds he planted with us.

We were content, and we passed the years. In '75 we got the parcela. Those years were peaceful. In '79, the problems from the armed conflict began. They started to kidnap the *catequistas* (catechism teachers), and the army started to turn people against the late

Padre Bill Woods. That was their plan, definitely, because around that time, the colonels were offering to give us help like cardamom dryers and coffee bean huskers. Some places accepted these, but many didn't; they didn't trust the army, or there were strings attached.

We were developing. Some of the people had produce or livestock (to sell). It wasn't a lot—a few cows, some cardamom, small stores. The co-operative was developing. That motivated the army to come out against us.

Maybe the guerrillas were penetrating the area, but we didn't know. The soldiers didn't tell us. They ignored us. They thought that we were collaborating, or that we were guerrillas. That's how the troubles started.

In 1980 and '81 is when the massacres began, the scorched earth. Here in San Lucas, at the Fourteenth Center, Cuarto Pueblo, at all the five co-operatives. The massacre in Cuarto Pueblo was the biggest. It was a Sunday, a market day, and all the people were in town when the army came. That's where it was the worst. When we found out what the army did—kidnap the people, massacre them—we fled to the jungle. Because we fled, they didn't kill us. If we hadn't left, they would have killed us for sure. They killed so many people.

We didn't know how we were going to live. Some wanted to leave, some left only at night [when the army would take people for execution] and returned to their homes by day. But the army was capturing people on their way to Cuarto, to Los Angeles. They passed close to us, but the children were quiet. We went by Cuarto and saw that the people were burned. Some who saw what happened and escaped told us what was going on. They were killing the children, the women. They enclosed them in the churches—both Catholic and Evangelical—and in the clinic, in the office of the co-operative, and they burned them. They took the children by their feet and broke their skulls against the beams of the houses. So how could we stay in our communities? What happened in Cuarto would happen to us. What was there for us to do? We had to go into the jungle. The army said we were with the guerrillas. We had to go. So from 1981 or 1982, we lived in the jungle.

Our *compañeros* (in Ixcán Grande) were organized by centers. My neighbors in the center where I lived—there were thirty of us—all went into exile. I don't know where they are—if they're alive or not. They didn't come back to Pueblo Nuevo. And the directors of the five co-operatives, I've never seen them either. I don't know if they're alive or dead.

My wife was pregnant when we fled. Eight days after we went into the jungle, my daughter was born. We were fleeing, and eight days after leaving home, my *señora* was bedridden. When one lives in his community, he can take care of his wife, take care of his house. But in the jungle, it was the opposite: We suffered, and the one who suffered most was my wife. There was no medicine, but in the end, the girl didn't die and neither did my wife. That birth was our first experience living in the jungle.

After three years, when the baby had grown, another child (a boy) was born. Three were born there—two boys and the girl who was born when we first got into the jungle. If the army came, we carried them all. They're still alive. My daughter is now a grown woman. We have grandchildren.

I stayed in the CPR (Communities of People in Resistance); I didn't go into exile. There were a lot of us who decided among ourselves not to go because, honestly, if we had to die, we would rather die here defending our land. We couldn't leave it. We decided to stay there. We resisted all those years until we came into the open. And here we are, united in Primavera—we who stayed in the jungle.

But the majority went into exile. They couldn't withstand it. They returned [to their places of origin] or went into exile in Quintana Roo, Campeche . . . . I don't know all the places they went, but they didn't come back. Some stayed on in Mexico as citizens. I have an aunt who is in Quintana; she's Mexican now but of Guatemalan blood. If I'd gone, I probably would have stayed in Mexico too.

Those of us who stayed suffered when we went into the bush. We didn't have medicine, we didn't have clothes, machetes, files [to sharpen machetes], especially medicine for sicknesses. Yes, we suffered, but we were learning how to live. We learned to plant crops collectively. The army would come and chop them down. They cut down the beans, the corn, the rice, everything we had planted. They took the bananas, the oranges; they shot the cows— all of this so that we would die of hunger. If they couldn't kill us with bullets, they would kill us with hunger. But we learned to eat the herbs we found in the jungle. We ate a bush called *jushte*. We planted *camote, malanga, yucca*. That's what we ate when they left us without corn. When the corn was small, about a meter, meter and a half, starting to flower, they came and cut it down. When it was dry, they burned it.

But we didn't die. They wanted to kill us, but as we had the things I mentioned, we survived. We had a type of *papa de aire*. That type of *papa* (potato), it weighed a pound when it was grown. There was *bijuco*, a type of green. It was good food that we found in the bush. We were without beans, without rice, without corn, but we had *papa de aire, camote, yucca, malanga, bananas, jushte, zapote*. With all of that, we were able to live —not just me but all of the people of the CPR. And there were a lot of people. That's how we lived for many years, totally hidden, running from the army, until we came into the open. When we went into the bush it was 1981 and we stayed there through '82, '83. '84,' '85, '86. The worst of bombardments came in 1986. They thought they would finish us.

The army began to bombard when they detected smoke. Our wives and our mothers, who stayed with us, suffered because they had to work at night. They got up at one or two in the morning to gather their eggs, their potatoes, their bananas, whatever they were cooking, whatever we had. If it hadn't fallen into the hands of the army, there was corn or rice. They had to cook it at that hour—at one in the morning, at two in the morning, at three in the morning. At four, they put out the fires. And the food was ready for the families to eat. If you didn't put out the fire, if there was still fire by five in the morning, then the army knew that where there [was smoke], there were people.

They didn't treat us as a civilian population but like armed forces, like the guerrillas. But who were we? We were children, old people, women, pregnant women, children one month old, just born—the products of humanity. That didn't stop. One kept reproducing. That's why they were bombing when they saw smoke. If someone had just had a baby and they had to leave, the baby was carried by another. We helped each other.

We named a committee in each group to keep on the lookout for the army. If the army came or was bombing, then we had another safe place to go, to save ourselves. We began to organize. We worked together. We put out watches. If the army came, we left right away, hid in the bush. We put guards far out from where the population lived. If the army came, they warned us, and we moved the camp. That is how we protected ourselves. In fact, one day there was a bombardment in the place where we had been, but we had just moved.

It was the same for all of the groups. We were all just saving ourselves. We helped each other. They never finished us off. Some fell, of the CPR, the population in the bush. In our community, three were killed—two women and a man. Others were wounded.

The guerrillas couldn't protect us from the bombardments. We hid in the trees, some of us digging ditches to hide in. They never hit us directly. They hit twenty meters away. But we were down in the trenches we had dug. When the bombardment was over, we came out. Once, someone started running, a helicopter saw him, launched rockets, and he was killed. They were able to kill three in our community. We weren't armed. We were civilians. The jungle protected us. That is how it was.

The dogs were killed, because a dog will bark. And the roosters . . . as we couldn't go without chickens . . . I don't know how they got the idea: They cut the voice box of the roosters. The roosters still crowed, but you couldn't hear it. You could hear it from about five meters away, no more. The chickens laid eggs, produced chicks. But the dogs we had to kill, even if they were good dogs. It was hard if they were good hunters.

We taught the children not to cry. When we first went into the jungle, it was very sad—the mother or father covered the child's mouth when they cried. Eventually, the children realized we were defending ourselves from an enemy, and they rarely cried. They cried out even less than the older ones. They understood; they resisted the urge to cry out. That got much better over time.

The children. What could we do with the children? Naturally, they had to study. There were many who could read a little, who had some education, had completed second or third grade. They were studying when the repression started. The children who had completed one or two years (of schooling) had been two years in the jungle. They were growing up. Eventually, we came up with the idea to see if we couldn't teach the children ourselves. But with what? There were no books, notebooks, pencils, or pens. We couldn't go out and buy them—we were surrounded in the jungle. . . . What could we teach with? We began by making tablets out of wood and using carbon from the fires. We had school up to the fourth grade, and eventually there were students up to sixth grade.

Another compañero had completed his training as a teacher, and taught middle school. I don't remember his name—he wasn't from our camp, and he died. He was the one who taught us. It began with that man, and grew and grew and grew until today—and look where we are now. Some who initiated the idea [of teaching the children] are teachers to this day

The children completed their schooling—grade school, fourth, fifth grades of school. If one of them learned, he taught the others. That was how we developed ourselves. Those who learned taught the others who had remained behind, and it went on growing. Now there is middle school and high school here.

That's how it is now, but it started with the charcoal. Writing on wooden tablets. The children saw and picked it up fast like a tape recorder. And when they took their exams, it was not with notebooks. They had to wash [their tablets] and reuse them. We were just talking about it last month. The children remembered their lessons and continued to learn. Like recorders, they kept learning.

For twelve whole years, we lived like that. It was like that when the priest Ricardo Falla came. He realized that there were people hidden in the jungle that no one knew about. They had heard stories, but when he saw it for himself, he offered himself up for these people—the poor, the Christians in the jungle.

After that, contact was made with the people in exile. Those in exile got support from international groups, got aid, schools, food. And us, we survived off of wild fruits, living in the jungle. We had to defend ourselves, but thanks to the padre, the path was opened. When they realized we were there, our brothers, our cousins, our uncles, came to us. That is how aid began coming into the communities of the CPR—through this padre. He said, "I made the decision to devote my life to you. I didn't know things would improve like they have. I came in thinking I might lose my life with you."

Schooling improved. We got notebooks, pens, and pencils, other resources like soap, salt . . . . Until then, we didn't even have salt in our food. There was none. We cut a brecha to the outside [meaning Mexico], and in 1992, we came out in the open.

When we first fled to the jungle, some went one way, others another. My father had been with me, but he went into exile. The time that I was in the jungle, my father went on not knowing what had happened to me. But later, while I was still in the jungle, he was repatriated—not just him but many—and ended up in Mayalan. He didn't return to Pueblo Nuevo. He got a parcela but was under the control of the army. He was there with one of my brothers, imagining that the army had killed his son, or that his son was a guerrilla.

Some of our people had been captured by the soldiers. They were brought tied up with a lasso, and the soldiers asked the people under their control, "Is this one of your family?" That is what my father told me when we made contact later.

"I was sure my son was dead," he said. "The army caught so many people—men, women—[saying] those are all guerrillas. 'Ya, we killed them; here they are,' they said. Afraid one was our son, we went to see, but you were never among them. . . ."

My father was in Mayalan for two or three years. First, they were at the crossroads by Veracruz, and from there, they went on to Mayalan. Later, my father came and lived with me another seven years in Primavera. I was content to have him here with me. We were separated because of the war, but we returned to live together. He and my mother died here. My father was a hundred ten years old, my mother ninety-five.

There has been no change. Perhaps now, the government thinks a little differently, that they won't do as they did before. But no, what we hear now is that there are martyrs. That is how it began in the 1980s. Only now, what we don't know is who it is that is doing it—before it was the army, the death squads, as they were called. It is starting again. We are not free like they say—there was a peace [treaty] signed, but there are many people dying still.

I don't know what will happen with this situation.

. . . There is still not peace for those who live here in our country.

Agustín Matías
Primavera, June 1, 2010

The violence . . . . It started when I was in school there in Pueblo Nuevo. In 1976, the problems began between the army and the guerrillas. I was in school that day. The army always came to the school to say that we shouldn't have anything to do with the guerrillas because they were Communists, that they were bad, they were like animals, that they would steal things, that they were violators of human rights and I don't know what else. We just listened; we didn't know anything about the violence yet.

Agustín Matías

Suddenly the other group, the guerrillas, came giving out fliers [saying] that the war had begun. [They wanted] to organize the people to join them. When I went to school, there were banners in the streets.

It got worse. The army began to control the people, the students, the teachers, those who went to work in their fields. They were checking to see if people were cooperating with the guerrillas. That is how the violence began. They began to kidnap people one at a time. There were military commissioners in Pueblo Nuevo, in Cuarto, in all the co-operatives. [The army was] very organized. The military commissioners were the ones who gave information to the army at the fort. If there was any movement, they reported it. Then the army would come to the houses to kidnap the people at night. In that way, people were disappeared.

Then the army gave some things to the people, gave *incaparina* (cereal) and cooking oil to show that they were friendly so the people would not go to the "other side." They offered books so adults could study. They let adults study, but it was only to see who they were, to collect names. In that way, the army began what they called the counter-insurgency.

They began with the members of the co-op and their children. Threats against the people began. People didn't know what to do.... [They just wanted] to go to work, not to be on one side or the other. There wasn't a big massacre in Pueblo Nuevo, but the army kidnapped the leaders and people that they suspected were organized with "the other band."

The guerrillas began small actions against them. The firefights began. They attacked the forts with rifle fire from one side or the other, harassing the soldiers. "They attacked us," said the army. Then the army would come out, and look [for the guerrillas] among the people. [The guerrillas] attacked a helicopter and downed it. It crashed in our center, Center Santa Rosa. For that, the army accused the people who lived close to where it fell of being guerrillas, of shooting down the helicopter. The army kidnapped the owner of the house, one Lucio [and] those who were in the house when they arrived. They didn't say anything, just took them to the fort, and the people were never seen again. From that day on, the violence got worse.

After the helicopter fell, it burned. The officers inside were killed. They were coming to talk to the people that evening. They were going to talk with all the members of the co-operative. But since they were shot down, they couldn't speak to the people. They were dead. Perhaps they spoke from the other world.

The planes came, the Arava [an Israeli plane], the helicopters, to bombard all the area. And as we didn't know about war or violence, it sounded to us like it was a fiesta. But where (the bombs) fell, there was fear, all the trees destroyed. They flew over the houses and machine-gunned. The A-37, a warplane from the United States, came to bombard us. They were rented or purchased. I don't know how they got them. They came from Guatemala [City] and bombarded us for two hours. And then they left.

The students were afraid that something would happen to them. Many resigned and did not come back to school. For those who lived far and had to walk, the army always appeared in the pathways, taking names, watching. So many students stopped coming to school. They came to say they wouldn't participate, that they were afraid of the army. That is how it began.

The teachers left for their hometowns in the year after the guerrillas shot down the helicopter. There were no more classes. The army came to harass people in the schools, to threaten them, to rape them.

The army went out at night dressed like guerrillas, went into the cafes and the stores, saying, "We are the guerrillas," with long hair, asking for free things. The people pretended not to know [who they were], because if you noticed, they killed you. In order to survive, people just watched and listened to what they said. Because if you paid attention . . . it was a trap for the people. They would kidnap or kill them

When they burned the co-operative, the army tried a tactic of entering hidden in disguise. They came into Chipal, to the north of the co-operative, near Cuarto Pueblo. They landed there about five in the evening. There were people about, campesinos, members of the co-operative. They saw the helicopters, that people got out, that they went in the direction of Pueblo Nuevo. On the trail, they camouflaged themselves to look like the guerrillas. They had long hair, backpacks, green uniforms.

We saw them pass in front of the house at nine at night. They had arms unlike the army's. But we had heard the helicopters that evening in the north. For sure, they were soldiers entering Pueblo Nuevo. In Pueblo Nuevo, there was no army [fort], just the people; some still lived there, some had fled.

Eventually they got to your house [where the pilots stayed], and began to tear it down. They came to the house of the agronomist Tonino that was on the edge of the town, and began to break the boards.

Later they got to the *tienda* and broke in the doors. Eventually, they set the houses on fire. We saw light from our center. They shouted, "*Viva el Ejército de los Pobres*" [Long live the Army of the Poor]. They yelled as if they were the guerrillas. "We came here to burn your houses," they shouted. On the walls of the houses they painted *Viva el Ejército de los Pobres, EGP* [the Guerrilla Army of the Poor]. They burned the market, the jail, the office of the co-operative. All was burned. They looted the store. They filled their packs with merchandise, took juices, soft drinks, everything that was there. What they didn't take was *laminas* [corrugated metal roofing], tools, sugar, salt. They couldn't carry it, so they burned it all.

The next day, from everything, the market, everything, there was only smoke rising. The people came to see what had happened, just looked on in silence. They couldn't say anything. If they spoke, for sure there would be "ears," spies, paid informers among the people. If you speak badly of them, they accuse [you]. No one could say anything, just look at what had happened. We knew it was the army because we saw with our own eyes when they passed. But we said nothing.

That same night, they left in the direction of Xalbal, on the road that goes to Veracruz. That is where they went with their cargo of merchandise. When they got to Veracruz, the trucks were waiting and took them to Playa Grande [a big military base]. Some people saw them pass by. That is the story of the burning of Pueblo Nuevo. That is what we saw. We were left without the co-operative [offices]. The hospital that the same colonel had built was destroyed. They threw grenades and left it destroyed. They left it painted *"Viva el EGP,"* *"Viva la Guerrilla."* They left that written on the walls of the hospital. Everything was destroyed, [even what] they themselves had built. The people couldn't speak out; it was dangerous for civilians. They didn't accuse one side or the other, just remained there. What happened happened. And so the people began to leave.

At that time, the army [fort] was still in Cuarto [Pueblo]. When they burned the co-operative [of Pueblo Nuevo], the army came from Cuarto. They said, "It was the guerrillas that came and burned everything. The guerrillas are bad people. You saw that the guerrillas burned your co-operative, the general store, everything. Go home and tell your parents what damage they did." That was the propaganda of the army. The people just listened. They got together on the edge of town, where the church is now, and the army said, "Yes, we came to clarify that the guerrillas did this. Did you see where they went? Where they are hidden?" Well, the people didn't say anything. They just stood there without saying anything. "We are not experts in these things," the people said.

The [army] met with the directors of the co-op and the mayors to advise them not to help the guerrillas, and that if the guerrillas came, to alert the army, "and we will kill them. We are here to defend the people, not to destroy. But it was they who damaged the town.

At five in the evening, they left in the direction of Cuarto Pueblo. [There were] about a hundred soldiers. As they were returning, the firefight began in the arroyo behind our parcela. Much shooting, grenades, machine guns . . . . We didn't know what was happening. "Run, you will get hurt." The neighbor from the next house wasn't there, just us. It was eight or nine at night when the fighting started.

Afterward, the soldiers came to our house, furious, angry. They entered through the kitchen door. "Hey *Señor,* get up," said the lieutenant. They forced their way in and began to check sacks of grain, under benches. "Are you guerrillas? Did you see them close by?"

My father said, "We are not guerrillas. We don't know about those things. Are they animals, dogs, cats, or are they people?"

"They are like you," they said. "They look like you."

My father said, "I only saw that a few passed by yesterday heading for the town. Maybe it was them. It is hard for us to distinguish."

"No, the guerrillas attacked us. They were hidden there in the jungle. Those were the ones who destroyed the co-operative." Those were the lies they told us. They wanted to take my father from the house. "We will check the house to see if there are hidden arms, things hidden . . . ."

"Go ahead and look. There are only fleas from the cat." They looked but there was nothing.

"Give us some water," they said. They were very angry. My mother gave them a pitcher of water. She had another jar boiling on the fire. If they tried to take my father . . . .

I, as I was little, I went outside. They had the door closed. There was a soldier in the doorway so no one could run from the house. I pushed the door slowly. If anything happened, I would escape or hit one of them with a piece of firewood if they did anything. If not, then [stay] calm . . . . The soldiers complained, "The guerrillas attacked us." They were there twenty or thirty minutes accusing [us]. Meanwhile, the other soldiers were looking around the house. Others were on the trail. They had a dead person, but it was someone embalmed. He had been dead awhile. They said he was a guerrilla with an old rifle.

My father said "We don't know anything about the guerrillas. Please leave us in peace. Here we work; we have our crops, corn, yucca, everything. We are not guerrillas; we don't know anything about them."

"Okay, *Señor*, stay with your wife, rest," and they left once again for the center [of town]. At nine at night, they arrived at the center. They had something with them, like a dry log, dragging it on the trail. There was a descent; the head banged on the rocks. It was a person they dragged with them, a cadaver. Who knows how many days it had been dead? The next day in the morning, they again gathered the people. "We were attacked by the guerrillas when we went in the direction of Cuarto Pueblo, but we killed one. We brought one dead, all dried out with hunger. That is what the guerrillas [look like]. They showed the cadaver to the people. He had an old uniform and an old rifle. "That is what the weapons of the guerrillas are like. Don't have hope in the guerrillas. We have good arms [which they showed us]. If you join [the guerrillas], you will die like this. They are not going to win. They are the ones who burned your co-operative."

Another neighbor, Viviano Calmo, one of his daughters was working elsewhere. He was the mayor then. He had fled when he heard the firefight. He saw the cadaver. He thought it looked like his daughter, her height, her weight. He accused the army of killing his daughter, "Where did you kill my daughter? Tell me, why did you kill my daughter? It is certain that you are the bad people."

That evening, his daughter appeared. "No, papa, it wasn't me. I've arrived from my work." He didn't say anything. He went home content that his daughter was alive, that she hadn't been killed by the army. He had been crying, thinking the army had killed his daughter.

The next day, the army returned to Cuarto Pueblo, having left word that we shouldn't organize with the guerrillas, that they are bad people, thieves, that they have long hair; they are animals, snakes, dogs; they are devils. We shouldn't put our hopes in them. But we saw that it was not true. When we were in the resistance, we saw that it was not true. They were people like us. That is how the burning of the co-operative happened, with lots of lies.

Later, there was the massacre at Cuarto Pueblo, in March of 1982 or 1980. I don't remember the year of the massacre. The army left Pueblo Nuevo and went toward Cuarto to live. They built their fort there. The guerrillas had attacked them at dawn. And later, the massacre took place in revenge. The people paid a high price for the attack.

The army had left Cuarto Pueblo and gone back to Playa Grande. The people were happy that there was no army presence, and then they [were] attacked on a Sunday. The army came from the Mexican border and entered through Chaculi, by the confluence of the Xalbal River and the Rio Lacantun and the border with Mexico. They advanced on Cuarto Pueblo. They killed a lot of people in Concepción, a center where people were gathered in the church, celebrating on Sunday. They were charismatics. They were there praying when the army arrived and told the people to go to their houses. But the people didn't pay attention. "They won't do anything; God is with us," said the people. But God wasn't important to [the army]. They massacred the people there in Concepción. I don't know how many families, but there were many. They were Jacaltecos. They were killed, the houses burned, the women killed, the children, everyone. They chopped everyone up.

From there, they came in the direction of Cuarto. Some gave warning, "Get out of here. Leave the town because the army is coming." But the people didn't pay attention. Those who were afraid and fled before the army came were saved. And those who stayed kept on with the market, as it was Sunday, market day. There they were selling, buying, playing football in the field. It was peaceful.

When the army came, they surrounded the town. They were on the ridges on both sides. The people couldn't get out. There was one path in the middle where people could go. When they realized that the army had come, some began to run. The army began to shoot at them, to massacre them. [But] the majority didn't run, they stayed put, thinking that nothing would happen if they didn't run. Of those who ran, some escaped, others fell dead, hit by the army's bullets.

It began. Children, women, men, evangelicals, Catholics, charismatics, whoever. They were all killed. There was nothing Christian about [the soldiers] that day. They killed everyone. For three quarters of a week, they had them, women, young people, raping them and killing them one at a time, until they killed them all. They burned them in ditches with gasoline and diesel, as there was diesel there for the [cardamom] dryers. They used that to burn the poor people.

It was not important to them if people were members of the co-operative. Everyone was killed, everyone was burned. Some were killed with machete, others with stakes, sharpened stakes like you would kill an animal. Even the military commissioners were killed because they were among the people. They were friends of the army, but there were no friends that day. The army killed them all.

People were dying. They killed the old ones first, then the men, then the women. Little by little, they were killing them. The girls were last. They killed everyone who had been in the market.

Some stayed alive, hidden in the bushes. They weren't found. The ones who [escaped] still tell the story about how it was in Cuarto, the evil.

That day, everyone fled to the jungle, those of Pueblo Nuevo, of Cuarto, of Mayalan, of Xalbal. . . . Everyone said it is better if we retreat into the jungle before they come to kill us.

The day the army finished killing in Cuarto Pueblo, they went in the direction of Los Angeles, capturing people in the pathways. The army didn't do anything to them, as though [the soldiers] were good people. And when they got to Los Angeles, they said, "We are not going to do anything. There is peace. We have finished the guerrillas"—as though supposedly Cuarto Pueblo was the guerrillas.

[The killing] was because of the attack on the fort. That is what they said in Los Angeles. "Relax, don't worry," they said to the people. But they also intended to massacre in Los Angeles. Some people were in their houses, others had fled to Mexico, others were hidden in the bush.

From Los Angeles, [the soldiers] left in the direction of Xalbal. In Xalbal, they again massacred the people, but it was more selective. There they [killed those] who were the leaders or [those] who had contact with the guerrillas. From there, they came to Kaibil where they killed more people.

Then a new government was formed. There was a coup, and the officers said, "Now it is another army. We aren't going to do anything." But the people knew. They left for Mexico. Others [were] in the jungle. The leaders began to organize to go to Mexico, to

Puerto Rico (a village in Mexico, just over the border), to Chajul, all over Mexico.

From that violence, the resistance formed in the jungle, the "Communities in Resistance." It began with small groups, center by center, those of Pueblo Nuevo, those of Cuarto Pueblo, those of Xalbal, those of Mayalan, all there together in the jungle.

Members of the co-op sometimes went back to their houses to gather their corn, their crops, but then the army came back and began a policy of scorched earth. They began to burn the houses, all the centers, all the towns. Kill or take the animals. The violence grew. In the area of the co-operative Ixcán Grande, there was only silence. Sometimes people went into the centers to recover roofing tin for their shelters in the bush. There was nothing to cover us, no nylon [sheets of nylon tarp]. The people organized in order to recover the roofing tin from the towns. Each one got two, three, or four sheets of roofing. When we got there, all the tin was burnt, roasted, the house of Padre Guillermo, the co-operative buildings, the market, everything was burnt. But even though it was burnt, we took [the tin], as it would protect us a bit from the rain.

The resistance began. We were in the jungle, but the army passed by on the trails, looking for people, looking for animals. . . . It was like that for a year. Then the army began a new tactic, going into the jungle, and it was even worse.

We were hidden in the jungle, and the army began to penetrate there. So the people began to run, to keep on the move. Before, the people just put out scouts to see where the army was, and they would retreat, to not fall into [the army's] hands. But when the army began to penetrate into the jungle, it was more dangerous. They could appear from any direction. So the people began to have scouts roaming all around to make sure the army wasn't approaching. There was one group of guards who were fixed on the trails that led into our camps, and another group moving, looking for movement, noise, in order to warn the people. People began to get sick. They had been in the jungle for a year without being able to get out. . . . The climate began to get to them. There was no sun, only shade, lots of rain, many mosquitoes, malaria.

But little by little, the people became familiar with the place. And the people kept resisting. Today they are still alive, those who resisted in the jungle. As the saying goes, "God was with them," there in the jungle, enduring. The army came into the camps, but when they arrived, there was no one. The people had gone. Whatever they found, they chopped up with machetes, made holes in the cooking pots, broke the corn grinders and machetes so that the people couldn't [use them]. They broke the kitchen utensils. Everything was destroyed so the people couldn't use them in case they moved back or came to look for their things. That was the tactic [the army used] to finish off the people, to break the resistance. But the people kept a reserve of food and machetes hidden in the bush. If they lost one, they had another. They continued working their plots, planting their sugar cane. Planting . . . .

When the army saw that the people were not defeated by what they'd done, they began to cut down the crops, the cane, the bananas. But people had prepared. If things were destroyed in one place, they had three more small plots planted somewhere else. If one was destroyed, they had another. They planted root crops such as yucca, *malanga*, and yams. If [the army] destroyed what was above ground, there were still the roots. They couldn't dig them all up. They just cut off the tops with a machete and quit. For example, they chopped down the yucca, but (we) returned for the roots. The people dug them up and had something to eat. They cut down the bananas, but there were more in another place. But there was no corn, not like there is now.

Because there were so many people, they couldn't all hide. Many wanted to go, and many to stay. [Of] the co-op members, the majority stayed, but almost half the people went to Mexico. There were refugees from other places too, from the sierra, from who-knows-where. They came fleeing the repression. One by one, they arrived and remained in the resistance. The people now in (the village of) Primavera are from different places, not just the co-operatives. They are from Mayalan, from Xalbal, from Pueblo Nuevo, from Cuarto Pueblo, from Los Angeles, from Kaibil, from the sierra, from different parts. Because of the repression, they all joined together in Ixcán. They couldn't live where the army had control. Then the army formed the civil patrol. They were the most abusive, the most violent. The patrollers were campesinos. They could go in the bush to hunt the people.

Because of that, many others fled to Ixcán [where] there was better vigilance, better control, more organization, and there was more room to move. For example, the areas of Mayalan, Pueblo Nuevo, Cuarto Pueblo, Los Angeles—all that was abandoned. Only the resistance remained, moving from one place to another. When the army came from the south [or] the east, the people moved to the north or west. There were warnings before the army arrived. When the army came to one place, the people retreated to another. If there was a surprise, the people had to leave running, fleeing with the children, with bags on their heads, a piece of plastic sheet to protect them from the rain. That is how it was in the resistance. When the army came, it was hard, very hard.

But the guerrillas were also hard on the army. They attacked them tenaciously. The army lost [soldiers]. Earlier, the guerrillas didn't have good weapons, just rifles and shotguns. The army had good arms. They defeated the guerrillas. But later, the guerrillas, I don't know from where, they got better weapons. They had flak jackets. They dominated the army. The army's helmets went flying, and then the army became afraid of the guerrillas.

Before 1990, things were more dangerous. [Later] the army was afraid of the guerrillas. They were no longer dominating. And so then the people, the resistance, began to feel more secure because now the guerrillas protected the civil population. The army persecuted the people as though they were guerrillas, but they weren't. They were a civil population with children, with women, with old people.

The guerrillas gave information to the people so they wouldn't be captured. If you fell into the hands of the army, you would die. The guerrillas attacked the army before they got to the people.

The resistance kept organizing. They made contact with some churches in Mexico in order to buy necessities, machetes, and cooking pots. Mexico helped the population in resistance a lot. Things were bought secretly. They didn't come in openly because there was also danger in Mexico. There was control by the Mexican soldiers. One couldn't move freely. But there were good people, civilians who thought about the people (of Guatemala). They had heard the bombardments, the machine gunning. They helped to buy and send things secretly to the resistance. That is how the people survived. They didn't have boots, machetes, cooking pots or clothes. . . . A couple of shirts were rationed for a year; a pair of boots had to last one year. It wasn't enough, but with these things, the people survived.

The army received help from the United States. More bombs arrived, more machine guns. Even some American soldiers arrived to participate. Some were very big, but because they were so big, they couldn't [easily] pass through the jungle. The guerrillas killed them. They withdrew and didn't participate further in the war. After a week, they were gone.

The guerrillas made staked traps—"Vietnamese style," they were called. [If soldiers] fell in the hole, they were impaled. So they were afraid and couldn't advance much. The army tied poles to their waist so if they fell, they didn't fall completely into the holes. But they still couldn't advance freely. They couldn't run after the people. Because of the traps . . . [the soldiers moved] slowly, slowly. . . . So the people were able to escape. The people ran. They knew the area. The army didn't.

That's how it went . . . the people surviving the offensives of the army. The army broadcast with loudspeakers from the planes, "People, turn yourselves in. We won't do anything to you. You will be free if you turn yourselves in." The people only listened to the yelling that came from the air. But they didn't turn themselves in, because it was certain the army was still at war.

There is much to tell you, but I don't remember [it all]. The people suffered a lot, walking in the arroyos when there was an offensive. They had to walk in an arroyo to not leave tracks. The water erased the tracks. The army moved in battalions, three hundred, five hundred, a thousand soldiers encircling the jungle. If they found the crops, they cut them down. If they found patches of corn, they burned them. If they found hidden clothes, they burned them. But the people were strong.

It was hard . . . the resistance, the army, the guerrillas. Finally, one realized neither the guerrillas nor the army was going to win. Negotiations began.

After 1986, I'm not sure what year, dialogue began between the commanders of the army and the guerrillas. Then the repression against the people calmed down. People could now go to Mexico and contact human rights [organizations], and through them, contact Guatemala [to report that] we were civil populations, members of the co-operative, that we weren't the guerrillas. The guerrillas were apart from us. Clearly they were defending the civil population, but we weren't armed like the guerrillas. We were like the population who was [in areas] controlled by the army. The people could now come out in the open, farm peacefully. The army still came to persecute but not so much. It was calmer; the repression began to diminish.

The multiparty international commissions [came] to see if it was true that [we] were civilian populations. They came in helicopters to visit. The people made clearings where a helicopter could land, and gathered to receive them. They spoke to the [representatives] that had arrived from Europe, the States, from human rights groups. That day, the people made it clear that they were a civilian population, and that if the army wanted to continue their war, [it should be] only with the guerrillas, not against the people who were [now] out in the open.

The people were still afraid because the army launched one last offensive in 1987 to try to finish off the people once and for all. But they couldn't, and so they lost their enthusiasm. Before the offensive, they bombarded a settlement called Chiquimula at five in the morning. It was renamed "Dos de Noviembre" because on that date in 1987, the army killed five families there.

The dialogue continued in Europe, then the peace [treaty] was signed.

In 1996, the people came out into the open. They began to de-camp, not live hidden in the jungle. Helicopters flew over, but they didn't do anything. There were international accompaniers who came to live [in Ixcán] from Spain, France. MINUGUA (the United Nations Verification Mission) arrived. The ONU (United Nations) came to record the violence in Guatemala. In that way, the popula-tion went public . . . working . . . [celebrating] their fiestas out in the open. People came, visitors, family members. We could also go out and see family in other places, to see who was alive or not. To ask who was alive in the resistance, in Mexico, in the highlands. Lit-tle by little, [we] could contact the other co-operative members.

Some had gone back to the highlands, others to Mexico. There had been much movement among the people. Since we were people of Pueblo Nuevo, we were going to return there. Monsignor Ra-mazini [Bishop of Huehuetenango] was going to buy land in the area of the Ixcán co-operative for those of the CPR who had not been members before. But when the [former] members arrived from Mexico, they said, "No, these parcelas are for our children. You look for other land, another place to go to. We don't want you to inte-grate with ourselves."

Commissions went to look in Barillas, everywhere, in Peten, to look for fincas that were for sale. They found a finca named San Isidrio and another called San José, another Santa Marta. These were for sale. And negotiations began with the owners. The owners said, "Okay, buy it. This is the price." But where would the money come from? We had to ask for help from the bishops, from the churches. The church of France helped with the purchase of the land. Caritas de Quiche and Caritas de France, they helped with the purchase of the finca. And so, [our CPR group] moved from the area of Ixcán to here in Primavera.

We had parcelas in Pueblo Nuevo, but many were afraid of the army. They had come to steal seed. It was better if we of the CPR stayed together. We are united still. We came, together with those people who had no parcelas [in Ixcán], and arrived here, still organized in co-operatives. There is a youth organization, one for women. There isn't one for the elderly because there isn't anyone to direct it. But there are organizations of women, of men, parents, fathers and mothers, teachers, human rights, of health, of midwives. There are many organizations in the community. There are directors who guide the co-operative, others who direct the community politically, the governor and the mayor. That is how the people are now organized.

But we still belong to the parish of Candelaria, in Pueblo Nuevo. We go there to participate. The catechists from here go there [to study]. We belong there.

That is how the story ends. That is the little that I remember. There is more, but we wouldn't finish in one day. It would be too much for the tape recorder.

Margarito Matías
Primavera, June 1, 2010

We went down to Ixcán on the tenth of May 1964. First I came to see the area. Many had said, "Ixcán isn't good; there are many animals, snakes, jaguars, *saraguates,* other monkeys, many other types of animals. That is what we heard in Todos Santos. But others had gone to Ixcán. My cousin Victoriano was in Primer Centro together with Padre Guillermo and Tomás Pablo. I went there to see if it was true.

When we arrived, how beautiful that place was. There were people, animals in the pastures. I went to the office of my cousin, Victoriano, and told him we had arrived. We stayed with his family, with the animals. I said, "I am here to look at the place, to wait for a parcela. I had another cousin in the Third Center. We went there with her. My plan was to come first and plant milpa so there would be something to eat when I came with my *compañera.* They lent me [some land]. I cleared it and planted corn. I was there about five months

The corn was sprouting when I left to get my family. I was in Todos Santos a week. Then I left with all my family and my animals. We left on foot. There were thirty people with all their animals. We arrived in the town of San Mateo to meet a truck. The truck broke down, so we were there for some days. We got to Barillas. From there, it was a long way. Because the group had animals, women and children and babies, we had to go very slowly. We crossed the Ixcán River; on the third day, we got to Primer Centro.

We put our names on the list. After six months, they gave us the

Margarito Matías

parcela. At first, I stayed in Primer Centro. From there, I went to plant milpa. I planted what we would need to live on. When I had crops on my own parcela, I moved there. I had my land in Pueblo Nuevo, on the ridge on the way to Cuarto Pueblo.

I knew [Padre Guillermo and David]. When Padre had a trip, he went in the plane to Huehue or to the capital. There was a pilot working with that plane. Maybe it was you [the author]. Padre Guillermo was first in the Primer Centro. Later, he went to Pueblo Nuevo and lived there, together with this pilot. We worked building the airstrips in Pueblo Nuevo, Mayalan, Los Angeles, and also in Cuarto Pueblo. But we settled in Pueblo Nuevo, in Centro Santa Rosa.

Later, in the year 1974, I was named a leader. Each center had a leader. I went to the meetings with Padre Guillermo and David, and with the directors of the co-op. It went well. Many people had come from the mountains to live there. In 1975, others arrived. Some stayed in Mayalan, some in Pueblo Nuevo. Center One, Center Four. . . . They all came for the meetings in Pueblo Nuevo They came to the meetings to learn what work [voluntary public work for the co-op] they would be assigned.

We had been fifteen or twenty years in Pueblo Nuevo when the violence began. In 1978, '79, before the army had a fort in Pueblo Nuevo, there were roving patrols. One couldn't go out at night or they would take your animals. They kidnapped some men there, and some girls who were about eighteen years old. They captured the directors of the co-op and killed them. We remained there because we were members of the co-op. I had planted various crops, I had built a house with a tin roof.

One day, my wife went to wash clothes and bathe. She saw smoke coming from the house. When she got back, the house was just ashes. They'd burned the co-operative store, the market. All the houses in the center were just ashes, just carbon. My corn was burned. Not only that but the things I had [inside]; my clothes were burned. I had two stone corn grinders. They took them or broke them.

I had my crops, my yucca, my pineapple, bananas, oranges. They began to steal the fruit, to pull up the yucca, cut down all the plants.

The soldiers left, and when they returned, they took wood and [thatch] to build their fort by the airstrip. When they burned our house, we took refuge in the bush. We didn't go far; we stayed close to our parcela. We were there twelve years.

We were hiding in the jungle when we heard about the massacre in Cuarto Pueblo. We went close to Cuarto. What a number of people had been killed! We didn't enter the town but looked from the ridges. You could see many dead there.

Afterward, we went to the house [at their parcela]. We suffered. We went to wash in the arroyo, but we were afraid. We felt someone was watching. We heard [branches] breaking in the path. The army was searching. I went and got all the clothes. I threw them in a coffee sack and hid it to one side. I took the chickens, a machete. There was a battle, a lot of noise . . . . We fled, breathing heavily like animals when they fight.

Domingo Esteban Francisco
Lucía Antonia Martín
Primavera, June 2, 2010

Domingo:
 I am from Huehuetenango. My pueblo was Santa Eulalia. I was sixteen years old when I arrived here in Ixcán. [I] met [Lucía] in Xalbal. I saw her in a field, looking for her duck . . . .

Lucía:

I lived in Xalbal with my mother. We were there when my husband came to find me. Yes, I was looking for my duck, and I saw this young guy. He was making signs, but I didn't pay any attention. I left. But little by little, we got to know each other. One of his sisters told me he had "thoughts," thoughts of marriage. I told the sister that I wanted to think about it. But later, I fell in love and I accepted him.

Domingo:

She suddenly said to my sister that I could . . . . She said that my father could come to ask for her from her mother. Just that. I didn't speak with her. I didn't say, "I like you very much, let's live [together]," or other things like they do now. No, I watched from afar but didn't talk to her about how we could live, how I loved her, how I saw her. We didn't talk about that. Just saw each other from a distance. We have this custom. Those who talked about marriage were the parents. My father went to ask. She said, "Yes." That is how we arranged things.

Lucía Antonia Martín

Lucía:

Six months [passed between the encounter with the duck and the wedding]. Our custom is that the mothers and the fathers, the four have to communicate and reach an agreement. And us. If we want [to marry], we have to say to our mother, our father, that, "Yes, we will . . . ." Or if we don't want to, we say, "No." After the parents come to ask, then we begin to know each other, then we can talk. When everything was arranged, Padre Guillermo married us in Mayalan.

We came to Mayalan, to Center Thirteen. We lived there for some time. He was working, some days with my mother, some days in Center Thirteen. Like that we made our way. We had little. We were new [to each other]. Walking with him, visiting the parents . . . .

Domingo:

I worked with David. He was the engineer who supervised all the work of the surveyors. He was the one who checked the measurements. He was an excellent engineer. I watched the [other] en-

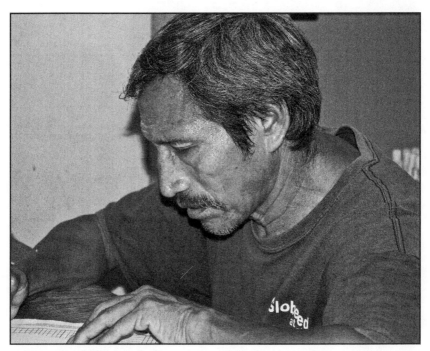

Domingo Esteban Francisco

gineers working on the survey lines. It always took them a long time to set up their instruments. But David, at the slowest, it took him [only] five minutes. We worked hard, running on the job. We did a huge amount of work with David. I knew him very well. He worked fast, and [the] work [was] well done. He was a good companion.

For a time I opened the brechas. I began to work on the runway at Mayalan, clearing the brush, leaving it more or less prepared. Then I went out with the surveyors. In Xalbal, we also cut down trees [and] constructed the runway. We left there and went to Pueblo Nuevo. There were various groups of surveyors opening clearings for the lines, so I just worked for a few days there in Pueblo Nuevo.

We had to search for [a place for] the runway in Cuarto Pueblo. We looked for a week or fifteen days to find a place for the runway. We checked various spots. If we thought we found a place, we measured it. If it was too short, we would leave it and look for a new location. Finally, we found where to put the runway, where the community is now. There was a good place on the bank of an arroyo. I remember it had about seven hundred meters . . . a bit more. We finished measuring that, then continued with a clearing for the line that went up to the Mexican border. We began to survey for the parcelas there. And after measuring the parcelas, I stopped working with the surveyors.

After I met my wife, I worked a few days planting crops. Then I asked for work in civil aviation. I worked for two years maintaining the runway. There was a military base. They had much bigger planes, the Aravas [an Israeli utility plane], helicopters, and others. Many apparatus that came from above landed there.

In those days, the wage was twenty-five cents [a day], but the government paid us 125 quetzales a month. I felt like it was a large amount of money. At twenty-five cents a day, in a month, one would make about five or six quetzales, but with the government, I would make Q125 in twenty-two days, with eight days' vacation. [A quetzal was $1 U.S. at the time.]

I knew the medium [size] planes of three or four passengers, and also the Arava, which carried a lot of cargo. [Bill Woods' planes] were small ones that carried four or five passengers. They left from Centro Uno and Xalbal, and went to Huehuetenango or to the capital. They carried out the sick, carried out the harvest and people from the co-operative. [Otherwise], to walk from Mayalan to Barillas took two days, and one had to carry a load of at least fifty pounds.

In the time of Padre Eduardo, there wasn't a rule [about how to become a member of the co-op]; a campesino [just] arrived. But when Padre Guillermo came, in order to know if a family really wanted a parcela, they had to be *ahijados* to a family that already had their parcela. [Ahijado literally means a godchild. What this meant was that the newcomers went through a period of probation before being accepted into the co-operative.] During the six-month trial period, the "ahijado" family watched [the newcomer]. The family had to report if there was a significant problem. Then [the new] ones would begin to receive their parcela. It was jungle—nothing had been cut down, not one tree. It was practically pure jungle.

I wasn't a parcelista; my father was. It was excellent land, very good. There was the Río Jordan. Father Guillermo named the river. The headwaters are in the Cerro Cuache; from there, it passes through the parcelas. At that time, hardly anyone had a pasture. They only planted corn and beans, rice, chile, bananas, and other things. First thing was cut down the jungle. One begins to clear in March, April. In March, one can burn for a month and a half. Then, one can plant corn or whatever seed. After that, when one wants to use the cleared land for another purpose, it can be used as pasture. But at that time, I think everyone had only corn, beans, rice, bananas. Later, they began to plant cardamom and café. Initially, it was good business. It paid well, but later when everyone had café and cardamom, the price dropped. When the price was good, a pound of cardamom was Q0.50 or Q0.60. And the coffee Q0.25 to Q0.40. But on the other hand, when everyone in the co-operative had these products, the price fell. I remember very well—when the violence was strong, a pound of cardamom was Q0.10. People came to Veracruz to sell their cardamom for ten cents a pound. It had no value. That harvest was lost.

As I understand it, the violence came to Xalbal . . . . The army said the people were guerrillas. The first violence was at a place called Centro Cuchillo. The army came and massacred the people. Many died. Before that, there were kidnappings and disappearances in the different co-operatives. We couldn't move freely; everyone was afraid. The army could appear at any moment.

[Then] for three or four months, the co-operative of Ixcán Grande was silent. The army left. They left Pueblo Nuevo, Cuarto Pueblo, Xalbal, Mayalan. The co-operatives were without any [military presence]. But a short time later, the army returned. That is when they massacred the people in Cuarto Pueblo. About three hundred seventy or three hundred eighty persons died there . . . burned, shot—children, women, and men.

At that point, the other co-operative members left. They went to hide in the jungle, abandoning their houses. Families began to leave because they saw that the army came to kill any people they encountered. We left Xalbal. We couldn't live in our village, in our community.

[The army] returned to look for people in Mayalan, in Los Angeles, in Xalbal, but they didn't find anyone. They burned the houses, they burned the co-operatives, they burned the churches, and also the animals. They killed all the animals that the people had, cows, chickens, pigs, dogs, everything. Everything they found, they killed. But the people were hidden on their farms. That is how the violence began.

Lucía:

As mothers, we suffered there in the jungle. We got up at two in the morning to cook, to make a fire, because we couldn't cook during the day. You couldn't cook because the airplanes, the helicopters would come to bombard. You suffered with your children. It was worse when you had a small baby. You couldn't put their clothes out to dry in the sun. One had to be careful how to take care of oneself.

If your clothes were out when the army came, they would bomb us, dropping big bombs, not the small ones. The army was always looking for ways to kill us. Our children couldn't cry. We had to cover their mouths so they wouldn't cry out. We had to be very careful of them. If not, if they wandered away a bit and were away when the army came, they would be killed.

For a pregnant woman, it was tough, hard to walk in the mud, in the water, very hard. I was living in the jungle when the army came to our community. They were bombing and shooting. Thanks be to God, I got out all right. It was the time of high water. I escaped with my first son, carrying him when I left. When I got to an arroyo, it was running, full of water where I [had to] go. [I thought] I would die. I had a child, carrying him; the army was coming, shooting, bombing, Thanks be to God, I didn't fall. Everyone running, everyone scattering, no one on a particular path, no one went together, everyone separately. I ended up lost. I couldn't find my husband.

I was alone, in the jungle without protection from the rain, without a mosquito net, with nothing, just the clothes I was wearing. That day, it rained hard. I pulled some leaves over me. The insects got in our mouths and noses. I used a stick to get them out. I was lost for a day and a night. I didn't find my husband. He thought I had been killed. I also thought the same [of him]. Just waiting for the arrival of the army. Thanks be to God, in that moment, my son did not cry at all. God helped so that he didn't cry. He ate some leaves, and had a bit of water that I found. He was a year and a half old. We were there in the rain, hungry, nothing to eat, nothing. The next day my husband found me . . . .

Because of the situation there, many women were dying. Many died from disease. There was no medicine. If you wanted to buy medicine, there was none. There were no doctors, no one. We learned about herbs. Those who didn't find herbs or medicine died. My sister died, two sisters-in-law died, my little niece, various from my family. They are buried there in the jungle. Many women died in childbirth. There were no midwives. Some managed to find a midwife at the time their children were born, others no.

I was pregnant, fleeing in the jungle with my children during a bombardment, when [my son] was born. My daughter, the one you see here, I was in labor with her on a day when a plane came. The plane was circling. I was in pain. All the family was in a trench, but I was with my husband. I couldn't think about it (the plane). At any moment, we could die, just hoping in God, that God would save me. If God said, "No," I would have to die. A man helped me. He stayed with my husband and me. Like that I gave birth, in fear. Perhaps the sickness of my daughter comes from that. I am also sick now, I'm not healthy, because of the situation we were in.

The other son, who is making tortillas [today] . . . . The day I gave birth [to him], the army came. The guards [warned us], "The army is coming." I left running. When we came to the place [where] we were camping, I slept. At that moment, the bleeding began. I was near death. When they saw I was dying, people came to help. The people were conscientious. They came to help me. If they hadn't, I would have died.

It was the fault of the army. If not, we might have had a midwife. We escaped by running. A woman giving birth should be careful, but that day, I suffered a lot. The same for other women. There were women who died, women who [became] swollen. Their arms and feet swelled up because of poor blood circulation.

One child was born during a bombardment, another while fleeing from the army, and another was a newborn when the army came and burned our camp. There was no rest. Some days in one place, other days in another. Each day we had to move. We couldn't stay in any one place because the army was searching [for us], bombing. We had to wait for the moment of birth, with lookouts . . . . And afterward, we had to run away, to find a place to hide; otherwise, they would kill us. I don't take long [giving birth], one hour and it was done. But not all women are the same. Some women [take] one hour, others two hours, some three hours, or there are women who [take] days. But I was always fast to give birth.

Often, there was no one to help at the moment of a birth, no one. We didn't have midwives, no health aides; there was nothing. Only with the help of other persons could we give birth. And for the other women, it was the same, no midwives and no health aides to take care of us—to the point that some women gave birth alone. Our health suffered from that. Me, I have problems from that time. There were no boots. We went barefoot in the mud. One got sick because there was nowhere to buy [medicine]; no money, no soap to wash clothes, nothing. We washed our clothes with sticks.

We had to defend our lives; if not, the army would kill us. They even killed the animals. We still had some at that time. My son, who just celebrated his eighteenth birthday, was a small child that day when the army entered. They killed all our ducks, our pigs. They killed everything, burned everything, our clothes, our corn [in order] to starve us. The army left us to die of hunger. But still, through the power of God, we didn't die.

We learned about the wild herbs, which ones we could eat. When there was no corn, there were roots of malanga, papaya, jushte. There were many plants that we learned to eat because of the situation.

My husband has family in *tierra fría* [the highlands]. His grandfather is there, his cousin, his uncle, the whole family, in Santa Eulalia. My family is in the town of Barillas, my grandfathers, my grandmother, my uncle, everyone. Now some still live in Barillas, in San Lorenzo. One lives in Pueblo Nuevo, one lives in Xalbal, one lives in Cuarto Pueblo, and one lives in Campeche, Mexico. They are dispersed everywhere. Some disappeared. I don't know if they are alive or dead. We searched for a brother of my mother. Only God knows if he is alive or dead. When the violence came, he left. No one knows what path he took. I am trying to find him now, but there is no news. We are sad because we knew him well. He was family; we lived together. But then the violence came . . . . Now, who knows if his wife is alive, if some of his children survived? Only God knows.

Domingo:

I learned a bit [about natural medicine] in the jungle, and later had formal training in natural medicine. Then a doctor from the University of San Carlos in Guatemala came and gave courses on pharmacy. I got my diploma and certification from the Ministry of Public Health. I can direct a medical pharmacy. After that, I studied natural medicine for four years. Then the Pastoral Social [a social outreach program of the Catholic Church] gave me a job. I have been working ten years now, giving consultations to the people and treatments with natural medicines.

Lucía:

Miguel, I remember when you worked with the late Father Guillermo Woods. You often came to Xalbal, to Mayalan. I've always told my children, I hope some day you get to know Miguel [the author]. When Padre Guillermo crashed in Xalbal, he suffered a lot. He was bloody when he arrived, but he didn't feel it. He laughed. "Don't worry, I am fine," he said. But he was bloodied from the accident. We were in Catarina's cafe. She brought a towel to clean up the blood. He was grand, the padre. All the women came crying, but father, bleeding, said, "Don't worry. I'm fine. No problem."

Father Guillermo Woods was a good person, I'll tell you why. My brother never grew, never developed. He was always in bed. My mother suffered much [because of that]. I was little, but I remember a bit. Padre Guillermo helped my mother. He gave her ideas about what might help the child, how to feed him, what to do so he might get better. When I was little, I walked together with my mother, carrying my little brother when we went to Mass, when we went to the *mercado*. After a time, she and I would tire.

One day, my mother began to talk with Padre. And Padre told her that the vitamins from crabs were good. "You should give [him] that to eat."

"All right," said my mother. She did it, because she wanted to cure her son.

"And also put egg whites on his knee to give him strength." Padre had a plan to take him to a hospital, but sadly, they killed him, and the poor child remained as he was. He died eventually.

Domingo:

I would like to say, because it is almost time [for me to go to work], that my wife and I are among those who stayed in the jungle. We left our house and stayed in the jungle from the beginning until the end. We didn't go to Mexico as refugees, nor to any other place. We stayed there in Ixcán Grande. For me, what she talked about was a strong experience. I saw war. I confronted it. I lived it. I suffered with my wife and my family. I have said to my children that we suffered great violence from the army, from the government, especially from the government of Rios Montt, but that thanks be to God, nothing happened to us.

[Lucía] had to remain alone because when we first went into the jungle, they made me responsible for coordinating the emergency, for moving the women from one place to another, [for organizing] the men who were farming. I was in charge of how to retreat. Later, I was named to the committee of the *Parcelaria* of Ixcán. [Lucia] had to remain alone in the camp [while] I was working with the camps of the [other] families, organizing food production, preparing for emergencies, distributing the food. As she said, there was nothing.

We had to make contact with the refugees in Mexico in order to get resources that the people needed. I worked eight years and four months as a leader of the Communities in Resistance. Because of that, Lucía was [alone] for much of the time. I spent six months in the Federal District [Mexico City] in Mexico to denounce what the army was doing, to explain the existence of the CPR in the jungle, and that not only the guerrillas were there but we were also there as a civil population.

Ana María Hernández Silvestre
Mayalán, June 10, 2010

I want to tell a story that came from my late father-in-law. We didn't understand it at the time. We were seated quietly in the corridor, and he began to talk.

"I am only going to be [with you] a short time," he said. "I am going to die, but you will remain and see everything that is going to happen. Listen carefully to what I am going to tell you.

"Ana María, you are going to a place far from here. A priest is going to buy land and divide it among the poor. You will go there. When the people arrive, they will be very happy. Suddenly there will be a war, and this war is going to last a long time. The people are going to be dispersed. [Some] will go to Mexico, each will search for his own way. Later when the years have passed, the people will return to their land again. But not everyone will return. Half will stay, and half will return. And of those who return, it is not known to where they will return."

I didn't understand. "Who told you [all] this," I asked him?

"It came to me," he said. "I know everything that is going to happen."

"Ah," I said, but I didn't understand. So I just said, "Ah."

I went to seek refuge under the trees in the jungle. [Later] sadly, I went to Mexico. I was there years, and I didn't understand or remember the words my father-in-law had said to me. When I returned from Mexico, I sat down here by the church with my belongings, drinking some *atole* (a drink made from corn flour). I was sitting there like in a dream, and I remembered the words he had said to me. How it would be, when I would return. I felt very bad. I began to cry bitterly. I returned alone. My husband had died. I cried and cried.

Later, I sat down with my children, and told them everything [my father-in-law] had said. It's clear the vision he'd had was correct. That is just how it happened. And so even to today, I don't tire of speaking [about it], because it's certain, everything the man said came to pass exactly as he foretold. That man, he had foresight, and I didn't understand what he had said.

But thanks be to God, he told me. . . . I always ask myself, "Why did he tell me that?" Maybe so I could record this. I will say to my children, "That is what he wished for." As he said it to me, I have told it.

I give thanks to God, and also to Padre Guillermo Woods. He gave us a piece of land to live on, to [plant] our milpas, and to have enough food. I am very content that he is with us. And also Miguel. We are grateful when you come to visit us. You stay in the place of Padre Guillermo. It makes us happy when you come to visit because during the years that you were not here, no one came to visit us.

The padre is among us. As he said when he was in a meeting with the catechists. "The day that I die, they are not going to bury me in my home town, nor in Guatemala [City], but here where I am sitting. Here they are going to bury me." He said that, and it came to be. He is in the church. We are pleased that he is here, because he is also our father. He gave us the land. He has done miracles. People in need, people crying in pain, people come to pray with him. Two or three times [when] people came to visit, to pray, they were cured.

And so thank you, whoever you are, who are hearing what I say. And thanks to God, that God blesses us, and you also.

I am from the *aldea* (small village) of Ichiwix. Our municipality was Jacaltenango. I was married with my husband, Julian, and I had two children when I came here to Ixcán: Bertola and my late son, Gaspar, the namesake of my father-in-law. Ah, *Dios Mio*, I don't remember when I came down [to Ixcán]. But I do remember that Padre Guillermo was in Primer Centro. Don Victoriano received all the people who came, enrolling them. He told us where we would go to live.

Ana María Hernández Silvestre

When we first got here, there was no entertainment. Nothing. It was sad. I lived on the hill above the village. We camped there in the jungle. There was no house. It was all jungle. Where the airstrip is was pure jungle. Nine months after we arrived, they began to build the market and all the [town] plots. They opened up the jungle.

Members of the co-operative came to excavate the tree roots to make the runway so that Padre's airplane could land here. At that time, he flew the airplane himself. It sounded sad when they cleared the forest, each tree "baaam, baaam." The men yelling and whistling. There were many men, but they couldn't cut down many trees in one day. There were lots of trees, and many were big ones.

A group of musicians had organized to buy a marimba. They were playing on the edge of the settlement where we were camped when we first came. When the men began to clear the land for the town, they got together to build a shelter. The *marimbistas* set up there and played while the people were clearing the jungle. Each tree that fell made a big noise. They were huge trees. . . . The marimba playing, the men making a big cheer when [a tree fell]. They were content, happy to see how the people worked. That day, Padre arrived in the airplane to see how it was going. He thanked the marimba players. He was pleased that they were cheering up the people.

After nine months, the padre said, "On this day, we will assign the parcelas." They were numbered. Padre took a man's hat, put in the numbered papers, and mixed them up. Each co-op member took out his paper. There they saw the number of their [town] lot and their parcela. Don David had divided up the plots, and so the people began to live on this hill. My husband played the marimba. He told Padre they were going to celebrate and play. Padre took them to Primer Centro to get what they needed. When they arrived back, they were all airsick. They had never been flying. They were scared, yelling, finally they arrived. But it made them laugh, and they celebrated the fiesta.

I knew Doña Mirna and David [Hollstegge], Juana, Jennifer, and Aimée. There were three daughters. I washed their clothes, carried the clothes to the river, and when I was returning with the basins of clothes, Padre helped me carry one. He always helped. I had so much clothing, and I was carrying Anita, my daughter. She was my baby. Mirna gave classes to the little children, so she didn't have time to also do the washing. I was the laundress for all of them.

The first child who was born to me here was Anita. Bertola and Gaspar I brought from my pueblo. The ones born here were Anita, Jorge Amario, and Luciano and Margarita. They were born here. Gilmer was born in Mexico. My son Gaspar died. I remember that day. Miguel, you flew him to the hospital in Huehuetenango, but we couldn't save him. He died there. That is how it was at that time

After Padre Guillermo died, we lived here a long time. The army was on the other side of the runway [in a fort], where the tower is now. The soldiers looked for places to go to eat. My husband was also very friendly. He was a good person, He said, "Okay, right here below is my house. You can eat there. My wife is there, perhaps she will give you tortillas." The soldiers came, all with their heads shaved. In the middle of the house was a cooking fire. They cooked their meat, and I gave them tortillas. I made tortillas, and they ate peacefully. One day my husband said, "Let's go to the parcela. It is hard to come and go; it wears me out, Let's go for fifteen days, and afterward, we can return."

"Fine," I said. But that day, the army went to the houses without warning, took people out, and killed them. They were looking for someone else but came to our house, and took [my husband] Julian. After they had killed him, they were talking among themselves. "Who is it that we killed? That man isn't the one we were looking for; it was someone else. This man is from the house where we go to eat." They hadn't checked to see who it was. Then they said, "Leave him; he's not going to live. Let's go," and they left. They left him thrown there. That man had done nothing wrong, the poor man. That is how my husband died.

In this center, all the returnees received their parcelas. Those who didn't return gave them to their children. My parcela is here, and this was my former town lot. Those from Xalbal and Primer Centro had to exchange theirs for others.

I have been a healer, and a midwife. It is a gift that was given to me. When my boy died, Anita was born. She was a baby when I began this work. When we first came here, there was no medicine, no store, nothing. The padre brought us our food. They made a path to the runway, and so we went there to receive [the food], to get what we could. We put together a little money. Quite a few of us were there on the ridge when a girl hurt herself. She was crying. How it hurt my heart. What could I do to calm this child, to get her to stop crying? "*Señora*," I said to her mother—Her name was Candelaria; she is dead now.—"give me permission to massage the foot of your daughter a little, to help with the pain."

"*¡Ay!, Dios Mío,* woman, go ahead. Do me the favor. My daughter hasn't slept for two days. Night and day, she is crying from the pain. Where can I take her for help? There is no one close by here."

"All right," I said. I held the girl, I hugged her a little, talked to her, then I began to massage her. Right away, the bone went back in place. That is how I began.

About being a midwife . . . I was asleep when my sister-in-law went into labor. I didn't know this. She was [in her house]. I was [in mine]. I thought I'd go to bed early; I was very tired. When I went to sleep, I had a dream, at about eleven at night. An angel said to me, "Get up. Don't hesitate, get up right now, get your son, light your torch, and go. I'll wait for you," the angel said in my dream. It showed me the way. "Here is a bunch of flowers. That herb will be useful for you." He put them in my hand.

I, in my dream, asked myself, "What should I do?" I was going around in circles in my dream. Suddenly I woke up. I looked around and lit a torch with pine pitch. We had made the pitch that day. We would light the pitch in order to walk at night. So I lit my torch. "Wake up," [I said to my husband], "I'm going. My sister-in-law was in my dream. I'm going to see her."

"What do you know? You ate too much beans and rice. You filled yourself too much, and for that you are dreaming. Be quiet and sleep."

"I can't forget my dream. I have to go." I got my son and a rag for a handkerchief and my torch, and left, walking. We went alone.

There was a bridge on the river. I crossed there, and was climbing up, when I heard a 'plak, plak, plak.'

It was my husband. "Where are you going?"

"I am going to your sister. She is sick."

"Ah, what do you know. You are going to drink coffee; you just want more coffee." He wouldn't believe me.

We were nearly there. "Don't say anything. It is me who's going, not you. Go on. I'll find the way by myself." And I went on.

Then suddenly "Oye!" said my [brother-] in-law. "Oye! Where are you going?"

"This woman says she had a dream, and because of that, we are going to see what's happening in your house. She says she had to go."

"Your dream is true. My wife is in danger. Quickly, let's go." We arrived at the house. Her neighbors were there. They were praying, as if she was going to die. I thought, "My God, where can we go? There is no hospital, nothing." But God showed me what I needed to do. And so I began. . . . And in fifteen minutes, the woman gave birth. In this way, I began this kind of work.

I learned a lot from Angela [a Basque woman who trained mid-wives in Guatemala and the refugee camps of Mexico.] I knew some things already. There was a meeting where we were asked what we knew. Those who understood should reply to their questions. Not everyone understood [the questions]. But I answered everything. They did an evaluation. After a while, they took me outside. "Where did you learn all this?" they asked.

"Even I don't know." Others had come out after me. We were three.

"Today you three are going to the hospital to attend births." It scared me. They took us, my daughter, a woman from Pueblo Nuevo named La Natividad, and me. The hospital taught us more. Doctor Jesús Comate Rodriguez was the head of the region. In a salon full of midwives, he gave me an award for my work. I was so embarrassed.

That is the story of those times.

Bartola Ross Hernández
Santa Elena, Petén, May 30, 2010

My name is Bartola Ross Hernández, daughter of Anna María Hernández and the late Julian Ross Montéjo.

I remember the Ixcán from when I was six years old, the countryside and the beauty of the place. The majority of it was jungle. There was everything. We ate fish, snails, shrimp, clams, everything that came from the rivers. A pretty stream passed just

Bartola Ross Hernández

below our house. It was fairly big at that time. We caught fish with a basket.

For vegetables, there was everything. In most of Mayalan, they planted taro root, kikeste, leto dulce to drink, chipilin, night shade, cilantro, every vegetable that you can plant. There was no problem; the land was fertile. In those days, there were no crop diseases. It was virgin land. Everything you planted gave forth; everything was very beautiful.

We didn't buy much plastic. We used clay dishes for cooking. When I was six years old, I worked the earth to make *comales*, crocks for tortilla dough, and cups. We fired them. We cooked corn in them. We didn't have things that you have to buy with money. We made them. Even hair ties, we made our own bands. We didn't buy bags. The people didn't buy much sugar either. My father planted cane, and from that, he made what we called "trapiche." With two pieces of wood, we pressed the cane. The cane went in the top, and the juice came out the bottom. We boiled the juice and got a pitcher of cane honey. From that, we made fresh drinks and sweetened coffee. On the farm, there were plenty of streams. My father planted on the banks. I watched him working every day. He also planted *café* and cardamom, which was the product most marketable at that time. For food, he planted rice, beans, corn, tomatoes, onions.

About the [political] organization . . . what can I say? It was very beautiful in that there was not much selfishness within the co-operative. I think that because the system, the co-operative, was multicultural, there wasn't too much egotism or envy. Everyone respected the elected president. It was a democratic leadership. [The president] explained what the pueblo would do. That was when I was six, seven, eight years old.

Ah yes, yes, [I remember] Mirna and David [Hollstegge]. I was very small, about six or seven years old. We washed Mirna's clothes. My mother carried the baskets of clothes; I took care of my little sister, Anita. Sometimes when we finished washing, Mirna gave us soup to eat at home. At that time, Mirna had her girls. Perhaps they were older than I, or perhaps younger. I can't remember their ages at that time, but she had two girls, and they were very beautiful. They lived near the airstrip, at the co-operative store. As you, Miguel, are with Gilmer [Bartola's brother] now, that is how David was with me, with my mother. When we arrived, he always called us over to talk. "Good afternoon . . . . ," he'd say.

(A pause. Bartola is crying.)

Also, there was another man named Tonino who lived nearby. He flew an airplane like you do. He was a good person. Tonino is a man who was old when I was young. My little cousin and I liked to watch when he came in with his plane. If we heard the sound of the plane from our house, we ran to the airstrip. When he turned the plane, we ran in the wind [of the propeller]. When he stopped, we were already there by the door. Sometimes he had a sweet. We'd go to the door of his house, and whatever he was eating, he'd give us a piece.

My parents had a profound love for all humanity . . . . In church, they played guitar, and at the town fiesta, they played the marimba. They had a band that played for the town. Every eight days, they played at our house. Anyone could come. It was free. The people were like a brotherhood. There were no problems. I don't ever remember a person being jailed or anything like that.

But when all "that" began, there were more problems. The army began to be a presence. There began to be a little more selfishness. Before [when] we had bananas or *plátanos,* we would go to sell them. People would buy from whomever. But later, it changed completely. People began to buy only from those whose parents were their friends and didn't buy from us.

I was eight when my father put me in school. I walked to school in Mayalan with a cousin from the farm. We were in Centro Estrellita, and being children, on the way home, we went swimming in the Rio Pescado and had something to eat.

One day, there was a grown man. Well, to me, he was a man, but at that time I was a young girl. Calculating as I see it now, he was about twenty-four, or twenty-six years old. He was swimming by himself. We were two, my cousin and I. There were other children, but they didn't stay to swim that day. Only we [two] stayed. By chance, we were there when the army crossed the *hamaca* over the river. I said to my cousin, "The army is coming. Finish eating and let's go."

My cousin said, "No, let's stay a while longer. Who knows where they are going?"

"Okay, I said." And we began to swim. They came down to where we had left our clothes and called the man. "Come here." He was from Zunil. They tied up his hands, and they tied our hands behind us. The lieutenant came and began to beat him in the mouth and the stomach. I will never forget that man because each time they hit him. . . . . When they began, he cried out. Oh, how he cried out. But after a while, he didn't make a noise. He was bruised, white, white and purple. I tried to look away, but they hit my face so I would watch. A soldier said to me, "What is happening to him will happen to your father if you tell him."

We had no choice but to watch. Then the man's eye began to swell, red, red from so many blows. He died from the beating. After he died, they let us put on our clothes and they took us to the hamaca. They walked to the middle over the river, and four of them began to swing the man. "The fish are going to eat him," they said. And they threw him in the river. "He drowned," they said. After that, they let us go. We were afraid; we ran.

Normally, it took us an hour and a half [to get home]. As we were children, we had to rest. But that day it took us half an hour. We ran . . . . When we were close to the house, my cousin said, "Let's stop here, catch our breath, so that our fathers won't notice."

"All right," I said. We were on the last hill before going down to our farms. We saw the army behind, following us. So we took off running again until we got to our houses. We didn't say anything to our fathers. I got sick. I couldn't eat, perhaps from so much fear. They took me out of school. When I was ten, I went back. I went through all that so that they wouldn't kill my father.

As time went by, it got worse. When I was nine and a half, the army took away the machetes of all the men who worked in the parcelas. They took them to their fort. They said it was because the work that our fathers did was to provide food for the guerrillas.

A man was taking a sack of corn to Mayalan. The soldiers cut a hole in the bag to see if he was carrying arms. The corn was falling onto the path from the hole. When he got home, there was little corn left. There was a time when they didn't permit the people to go to work. From then on, it got worse and worse. No one could do anything. Until, when I was eleven, I felt I couldn't go on.

When my father died, David didn't live [in Ixcán]. I don't know if he knew [what happened]. I don't know. . . . Well, our life was like that. It is a very long story. When the war started, when they killed my father—they killed him the thirtieth of November of 1980. My birthday is the twenty-ninth. He was killed the thirtieth. That day, they destroyed the entire co-operative. There was no more co-operative in Mayalan. Six months later, [people] still wanted to return and rebuild the co-operative like it was before. It had been very *alegre*. All the members of the co-operative would come for fiestas. They would elect a queen, the Queen of the Jungle. It was very beautiful, all the different cultures, everything. They had a big fiesta. Everyone was invited. They wanted to do it again six months after the death of my father. But they could never do it. Because of the fear that there was in that place, they could not return.

When I was eleven, the army retired from Mayalan. [They] left from all of [the Ixcán]. Only the military commissioners were left. They left six months after they killed my father. They were going to begin to massacre the people.

The sixteenth of March 1981 was when they [began]. . . . There was killing in all the co-operatives, and the massacre in Cuarto Pueblo. They burned everything. In Mayalan, they burned the generator, my father's marimba. They destroyed everything. They didn't leave anything. And after that, still in the same year —1981, in the month of August, or maybe a little earlier, in June—we decided it was better not to stay in the house, because the army bombarded the houses. If they saw a bit of corn, they would drop a bomb on it and burn the corn, burn everything. What we did was to take refuge in the parcela. We lived as refugees for six months, working in the parcela. Until one day … I don't know if from the helicopter they saw milpa, something, they landed. They cut down the milpa with machetes. We were campesinos. We ate corn and beans. That's what we lived on. We didn't have money. One couldn't continue living there. We were obliged to walk and walk. I walked a lot, as did my little brothers and sisters.

My mother was seven months pregnant with my little sister Marga [Margarita]. When my mother gave birth to Marga, she was in shock, She had lost her stability as a woman. It fell upon me for eight months, more, nearly one year, to be father and mother to my five brothers and sisters. I was only twelve years old. Anita was only six. Luciano, the boy who is also here [in Santa Elena], was sick. He couldn't walk. I had to help everyone. I got up at three in the morning. I had to look for roots of papaya, find a bit of corn, grind it, and make tortillas. And when there was nothing to eat, I went into the jungle. I looked for bananas, fruits, *chicos*. There was a red fruit, nice and sweet and spongy. I picked the fruit and let it ripen for when they were hungry. At times, I gave them just one thing to eat. Other times there was something else to add to the little corn we had. Sometimes I only cooked yucca, or we cooked sweet potatoes to add to the food. My mother couldn't even help me cook or help in the field. Because of that, we suffered much more than others. They had fathers and mothers, and they could move around. If they came to a place where there was corn, they stayed there. But we had to stay in one place because my mother was so weak and we were all so small. When Marga cried, we put a rag in her mouth so she wouldn't [be heard]. We'd also put a rag in Luciano's mouth. Later, I got the idea of putting the children in a hole and covering it with some wood so the army wouldn't hear them. When they stopped crying, I took them out.

We didn't have any soap. There were no markets. Everything destroyed, there was nothing. There was nowhere to buy soap.… There was an herb with a large flower. With that I washed clothes. I washed everything with it except hair. There wasn't anything to wash your hair with. Later, one of my aunts told me, "My daughter, you are smart; help me make soap. Go and look for ashes where they have burned the brush." I was happy, and filled a coffee bag with ash. My aunt began to add it to water in a bucket. With the bark of a tree, we made a tube. The ash paste ran down through it. She then killed a small pig and put it in the pan. "Add this to the water."

I said, "No, then we won't be able to eat it."

"It is for the soap," she said. I went to get water from the stream. We poured it on the lye paste from the ashes. We cooked it for three days. When it was at the point of boiling, you had to stir it so it wouldn't stick. I was little, and it was hard to stir, very stiff. At that moment a helicopter came. Miguel, if a helicopter saw smoke, it would bomb us.

We ran. My mother ran one way with Marga. Jorge and Anita another. I ran still another carrying the pan of hot soap. It was so hot I left it under an *achiote* tree. Of course, the helicopter could see me. It followed me for maybe a kilometer and a half. I had a child on my back. I ran with him. I was just a girl. I could see the helicopter, the helmet of the soldier. He moved his hand, and shot at me. The child couldn't run; he just held on to me. The helicopter went here, and I went there. I hid behind trees. Because I didn't leave the child behind, [it was able to follow me more easily]. When I got to a place where there was jungle, the helicopter climbed up and lost me. Then they began to bomb me, shoot and bomb. I hid with him in a big tree. Finally, the helicopter left. Maybe they thought they had killed us, or it ran out of bombs. Who knows?

Slowly I crept out. The child, maybe from fear, he didn't cry. Then I saw his stomach. From beside his rib, blood was running down his leg. ¡Ay! *Dios Mio,* Oh my God, I said to myself. He is going to die. What will his father say? Now what do I do? If I tell him, he will cry, because of the blood. If I don't tell him, he will faint. He will die. I thought the bullet had entered his stomach. Because I'd held him so tightly, he hadn't felt it.

"My son," I said, as I looked for the bullet. Because of the blood, I still thought it was a bullet. "My child, let's go in the stream. They won't kill us now."

"I don't know," he said. "Let's eat something."

I said, "Okay." A small bird was singing beautifully. "Look at the bird. I don't know if it is singing from fear, or if it is singing because it is happy we didn't die, or if it is singing because it is hungry."

"Maybe because we didn't die," he said. "Where is it? I'll look for it." When he was looking [for the bird], I threw water on him with my hand. "Don't get me wet," he said.

"I'm getting you wet so it won't see us," I said. I took down his pants and washed him.

"What is it?" he asked.

"I just want to see."

He saw the blood and said, "I'm going to die."

I said, "No, no, no." It was a stick.

"So I'll live?"

"Yes, you'll live," I said. A big piece of stick remained in the wound. "Look at the bird, he has hurt his foot." When he looked, I pulled out the stick. Afterward, the bleeding wouldn't stop. There was nothing. What could I put [on him]? Nothing, nothing, nothing. What [I worried about was] his bleeding. It never stopped. I put some leaves on the wound. The first ones I held on with my hand. The bleeding didn't stop. I put some on another place, and the bleeding slowed. I held them there, tore off a piece of my shirt and tied it [around the wound]. "There, now it won't bleed," I said. "Good." I washed the blood from his pants, and we walked on. We were lost five nights. I felt I might never find my mother. For five days, I looked. Nothing. She had returned with my uncle who was familiar with the farm. They went to look for me by day. But they couldn't find me. They were looking in one place, but I kept moving away. They looked toward the north. I went more to the west. Finally, I came to a path I knew. It took me to the parcela. There, I ran into my uncle. We hadn't eaten those five days, not even the child. I never felt thirsty. I didn't feel hunger or even fear.

I was twelve years old.

From that experience, I learned that that leaf helps [stop bleeding]. And after that, I began to learn about the herbs. I like it very much. Here, I teach a lot of people about [medicinal] plants. That is how it was for us at that time. Today, I can't bear to hear a helicopter. If I hear one, the day is ruined—the same with gunshots. Even if it is just a youngster [with fireworks], I can't sleep.

[It went on] like that until my mother got a little better and we could walk to Mexico. When we [went], I carried the clothes for all the children, and mama carried Marga and a cooking pot. She was still sick. [In] Mexico, the situation was even worse. The whole world was going [there]. I went first to see if there would be room for us. Then I came back up to get my family. We went down to Mexico in the second group.

We were walking through the pasture of Antonio Sánchez. I thought we were not yet in Mexico. I said to the men. "Be quiet, be quiet. The army will catch us and kill us." They laughed.

I remember Faustino Sánchez and Gregorio were bringing in their cows in the afternoon. They said to me, "Catica, what are you doing here?"

"No I am Bartola. But let's go. Run, the army is coming. They will kill us."

"No *chamaca*," they said

I said, "Let's go, let's go. I am going with my family. We can walk."

"No, Cata, let's go to the house." I remember that they gave me a little milk, and the señora called me "Cata." Her daughter had just died fifteen days before. She had looked like me, she even had short curly hair. So the señora, thinking of the child who had died, treated me like a daughter.

So, in this way God helped me. I was an orphan, and we carried nearly nothing. Everything had been burned. These people gave us some plates and a gunnysack of corn. After three days, they took me to the Mexican army. All the refugees were sick, there was no food, there was nothing. The armed forces of Mexico were the ones who began making tamales for the people to eat. They gave me an injection to calm my nerves. They told me not to worry, that they would take care of us. I thought they were injecting poison to kill all of us. Later, they said, "You are afraid, but don't worry, we will take you back in a launch." At one in the morning, they finished making tamales, and then took me back to my family.

Day after day, more people arrived. Week after week, there were more refugees. The time came when they couldn't support us. We had to go to a refugee camp. We were given a kilo of corn for fifteen days for each family. There were six of us. We couldn't survive. Because my mother was better, she made the decision that we would return and live in the parcela once again. Back to Guatemala, because even though we could only gather herbs, at least people could survive. On the other hand, in Mexico, everyone was getting worse. The men who took care of their children went out to get herbs, or to work with the Mexicans, to earn a bit of corn. But us . . . . So my mother said we would return to the parcela again.

That was in 1981. We went back to Guatemala. We were there for three or four months. Finally, we couldn't stand it anymore.

We could find a few plants, but we couldn't withstand the bombs. Night and day. We had to keep our mouths open during the bombing or we would end up deaf. I have two cousins with that problem. Maybe you know them. Don Sebastian Hernandez, from Mayalan, his two daughters became deaf. I say it is because of the bombs that fell. They are deaf and dumb. Because they were very young, [they didn't know to keep their mouths open during the bombing].

We went down [to Mexico] again in 1982, in the month of March. We couldn't live [in the Ixcán] anymore. When we returned to Mexico, there was more aid. In the Diocese of San Cristobal, all the Catholic churches were helping. There, I joined the administration because the priest from the diocese said that I should help the people. We made a storage place. We coordinated to divide up the food. I began to work as director of the kitchen for the malnourished children. We went to Quintana Roo. We were still there when the returns [to Guatemala began]. We also returned, but I didn't go to Mayalan because, as I told you, I can't . . . I can't be there.

Mayalan was really beautiful in comparison with how it is now. [It] was full of fruit trees. Now everything is bad. When Mayalan was destroyed, the army was ordered to cut down all the trees. And the land is not of the same quality as before. I don't know if this is because of the bombs that knocked everything down. They bombarded a lot, and for some reason, the land lost its fertility. I don't see bananas like there were before. I go to the coffee areas, and I don't see coffee beans. The white mushrooms that grew there, one doesn't see them anymore. You don't see even one hole [where they dig clay for pots]. It is as though the people have forgotten everything that was.

At times, I think of the people who lost their lives for this land. I am pained to see everything that happened . . . .

I returned with the refugees to the Unión Maya Itza here in Petén. But I had problems. I separated from my first husband. . . . I had problems because they didn't . . . maybe they never wanted me. Who knows? It was always a problem to live there. My mother gave me [away]. I had to be there. But I saw that I couldn't go on. It was better for me to leave. I separated from my husband, and I began to save my money.

After seven years, I bought this piece of land, a cuerda, no more. Even so, it is difficult. Hilmer is here doing his studies. I have my brother Hilmer, and Edgar, the son of my uncle. And my daughter also; I have one daughter.

Because of that, I didn't look for another companion. Better to work and help them study. What I make goes each month into what they eat, what the teachers ask for, and everything. They go on trips; the teachers say they are going and we must provide for everything, the lodging, the food. Here, you can't find jobs that allow one to work and study. Work is hourly. One can't do it. This year, I got a little ahead because Edgar finished his studies. He got a grant and went to Cuba. He'll study there for six years.

It has been hard for me because I didn't have another companion. I had to buy food. I had to work. I had to come home to [check on them] since they were youngsters. I had to tell them what to do; otherwise they wouldn't do anything. It was a headache for me.

Last year, I worked for the World Lutheran Federation. A man from the United States named Philippe Anderson had confidence in me. From when we first met, he called me "Bertolita." In my vitae, I always say that I don't have an education, but I have the capacity to work. It is from experience, not from book learning. He said, "I prefer those who are self-taught more than those who are school-educated. They are the ones who work the hardest."

"If you give me work, I will work hard," I said. I worked there and made Q4000 a month [about $500]. I could now save a little.

One day while we talked, I told him the story of the war. He then said that there was going to be a trip to Cambodia. "I want you to go and exchange experiences with the people there because of what you lived through. Your mother was pregnant and disabled. You took care of your brothers and sisters. You figured out how to feed them. You were orphans, and you didn't give up on any of them. Even today, you are helping your brothers. You haven't given up. Those people are recovering from a war. You can share your experiences there."

"Where is Cambodia?" I asked.

"On the other side of the world," he said. "We'll send you."

When he said the trip was on a plane, I was afraid. But he said, "You'll go with me, seated with your companions. There will be five of us." We went to the city. Philippe was the coordinator. One was from Nicaragua, one from San Salvador. We were six in all. So I went to Cambodia to share my experience in the war.

It wasn't fun. One can say that the only difference between a massacre and genocide is that here in Guatemala, there was more fear. Whether you admit it or not, you are afraid when they bomb from a helicopter, shoot . . . . On the other hand, over there, no. They tricked the people. And when they got them [to the camp], they cut off their heads. The people crouched in a hole, and they cut off their heads. The heads went rolling, and the body went . . . . They weren't living in [constant] fear. That's the difference. They were told that they were going to another place where there would be opportunities for them to study. So off they went. When the trucks arrived, the people stood in line, not to fill out documents but to die.

That's the difference between genocide there and [the massacres] here in Guatemala. Here in Guatemala, there were massacres; there, they used trickery. I went out to see where people died, struck by a bullet. For those killed, it is the same. The causes here were the causes there.

I was a child [at the time of the violence]. I asked a thousand questions about what had happened, about why the people left, about the bombs, about the war, the effect of the bombs. At times, I am, perhaps, a bit crazy. It all affected my relationships a bit. I am confused, and at times, I think perhaps it was not like that.

The type of leaders that there is now cannot be compared with those who were before. Today, there is not the brotherhood that Padre Guillermo taught. Now, people look to God but only with words, not from the heart. There are many bad things. But as I say to the youngsters who I have here, "God is everywhere. God is with one when he acts well."

I spoke with all my brothers recently about deciding whether to sell my father's parcela, because we can't . . . . My mother is old. I am here. I can't go back to Mayalan because . . . I can't live there. Everything that happened before, it causes me so much pain. I can't sleep at all when I'm there because I saw everything. I can't be at peace. It comes back again, even when I am here. When I remember my father, the people who were killed in front of me. Everything comes back to me, and I can't control my thoughts. No . . . I can't be there in Mayalan.

That is my story.

Alfonso Monzón Martínez
Mayalán, 2010

My name is Alfonso Monzón Martínez, native of Huehuetenango. From San Pedro Necta, Los Alizos.

In the year 1965, we came down to Ixcán. The first step was to come to see it. We didn't know where we would stay.

We were in La Máquina, renting land for planting, but there were people talking about coming here [to Ixcán] and they told us that someone was giving out land, a priest. That was Padre Eduardo.

We came all the way from Barillas on foot. It was far, more than twelve kilometers. Only on paths—there was no road. Many people helped and encouraged us.

It was very difficult. We brought many animals—chickens, ducks and who knows what else. All thanks to the late Juan Geronimo. He was missing a hand—he wasn't complete—but he had five mules that were coming up from [the Ixcán]. We said we had cargo, that we didn't know how we would go.

"Don't worry," he said, "I will take you and everything you brought." He loaded his mules, and that's how we came here. The journey took two days. One day we came down to San Ramón, where we stayed overnight, and the next day we left there and arrived at Primer Centro [the first center] at five in the evening.

That's when we met the late Victoriano Matias. He told us to go to Xalbal, but that was not easy. It was very hard to get there. [But we said,] "Let's go, it will be wherever it will be. If we are going to get land, let's settle there. That is where we will live." And that is how we kept up our spirits. But we couldn't go to Xalbal because there were still no paths cleared. We had to stay for a long time [in Primer Centro].

There were people living in Center Twenty (later renamed Mayalan). The families of the late Gaspar Alvarado said, "Come with us." We did not want to. But Padre Eduardo said, "Go ahead. There will be a town there. You will be close to the town. Go and look. If you like it, good. If not, continue on your journey."

When we came here, they had planted many crops. They had beans, corn, everything—tomato, heart of palm. Everything was bearing fruit. We had seedlings to plant but not a lot, so we returned (to Primer Centro). But we began to plan on living in Center Twenty. It was close—two hours walking from Primer Centro, the only place with a plaza where we could come and make purchases. So that is how we came. We are now Mayalanses.

At that time [the co-operatives] were still being formed. In the beginning, Victoriano was an administrator. There wasn't a board of directors. He administered the project, the distribution of the land, and Padre Eduardo worked with him. I was one of the directors here in Mayalan. The president was the late Pascual Morales, the vice president Francisco Carrillo, treasurer Tomas Pablo, secretary Jesus Camposeco, and me as spokesman. Five [co-operatives] were formed.

Chico Carrillo is still alive. He is in Mexico, above Pico de Oro, somewhere near Bonamerito. He didn't want to return. Jesus Camposeco, I think he is in Chimaltenango. I don't know exactly where. Tomás Pablo is living in Todos Santos. Pascual Morales, they killed him in El Quetzal. He is buried there. All because of the same storm that happened [later].

So the directorship of the co-operative was formed. We began to travel to Guatemala City to petition that they give us titles, that they give us some security [for the land ownership], something in writing about the land. At that time, it was very difficult. There was one document that Padre Guillermo said to complete. It said the land of Malacatancito up to the border with Mexico—from the Rio Xalbal to the Rio Ixcán—would be [reserved for the co-operatives]. The co-op directors took this paper to INTA (Instituto Nacional de

Alfonso Monzón Martínez

Transformacción Agraria, the National Institute for Land Reform). This was in the 1970s.

In 1976, we spent one month in Guatemala City, returning over and over again to INTA. We were always there asking, but they never attended to us. Afterward, Padre Guillermo came and said to us, "Have [the land titles] been approved?" We told him no, and he said, "Let's see if you've been to INTA to ask about this or not."

We said, "We've been there. If you like, let's go tomorrow." We arrived and met with a Licenciado Conrado in the entrance of INTA. We entered and greeted him. Padre asked if we had been coming there.

"Yes, Padre, they come daily."

"And you people here, do you have the hearts of Christians, or no?"

"Of course, of course we have the hearts of Christians."

"Then why do you keep these people here suffering? They came with two or three cents; some days they eat, and some days they don't. They have little money. They didn't come with enough money to eat. And you keep them suffering here, like it doesn't matter to you. Aren't they people just like you?"

"Yes Padre, but it isn't my fault," said the president [of INTA].

"But you have a voice. You can go and ask the man in charge to make this document."

"Yes, I have not done that, but I could do it."

"You are not children of God, because of the harm you have done to these people."

The lawyer was a bit embarrassed. We left. We went to other offices, to see papers in other places, I don't remember which offices, but it took nearly all day. When we returned at about four in the afternoon, the lawyer said, "Padre, your document is ready. They will give you the papers." So we went, Chico Carrillo and I. There was the document, complete. They had done it.

Padre said, "Lend it to me; we want to make a photocopy."

"That is prohibited," they said "Here we can't give even one paper. We can't do it."

"Can't you just loan it to me for five minutes, to make just one photocopy? I'll bring it right back." They didn't want to, but finally, they said, OK but bring it right back. We made seven photocopies. And then we brought it back.

We left, and Padre went to the center house of the Maryknoll Fathers. We went to the hangar that we had in La Aurora [the Guatemala City airport]. We were happy because it was a document that would help us very much. That was at the end of September. October passed, and then on the twentieth of November, they killed Padre Guillermo. They didn't let him live very long. It was as though they'd said, "We'll give you your papers, but we'll take your life."

Why do we say that the army killed him? Because at that time, the wife of the late Juan, who died in an airplane crash, was still around. ["Juan" (Jon Stork) worked as a pilot for Bill Woods. He was killed in a crash in 1974.] She was there; she would eat with us there [in the hangar]. An army patrol came to ask if Padre Guillermo had taken off. They asked where the padre was. We said, "He left, he took off."

"His time will come today," they said. They quickly turned around and went up [to the military base] for sure, to communicate. We later learned that around that time, the plane came down near Uspantan, El Quiche. We stayed waiting all that day, and he never arrived. That is how the death of Padre Guillermo came to pass.

It was very hard for us because we had a lot of support from him, we had a lot of faith in him. We suffered a lot from the disappearance of Padre Guillermo.

Today, there are many people who thank God that we got the land titles. That paper still exists in INTA. After the storm of war, they made individual titles. But by that time, Padre Guillermo had died.

When the violence began, people got very scared. The massacre in Cuarto Pueblo on the fourteenth of March meant the death of many people. It was a big killing. More than three hundred fifty or three hundred sixty persons, among them children, women, youngsters . . . everyone. Because of that, those of us who were here were very afraid and distressed. We saw that the army was going to come and do the same thing. When they burned the houses in the Fourth Center, we saw the smoke and began to look for a way to leave.

At that moment, there was a woman who gave birth. Her husband couldn't carry her because she was very heavy. And so we, my brother Archangel and I, said, "If you want to go with us, let's go. We'll bring your wife." We carried his wife, but then the helicopters began to come. We walked an hour on a path, then we stopped. We rested there a few days, but then the army began to surround [us].

It was very hard—everyone they met, they killed. They didn't leave anyone alive. I met my brother. He had been able to flee. But the army encountered other persons from the First Center and killed them. Nicolas Mendoza, he was killed by the army. One of his daughters was captured.

We went, fleeing for Mexico. But we were delayed because there was corn here, and we would have no other food. It took a long time. We were there in 1983 when the army came in and killed my brother, Clemente Gilberto Monzón. He was going to get a bit of rice from a storage shed that he had. He was returning when the army came up the hill where he was walking and they killed him. They fired their guns killing him. And so we left, we were very affected by his death. We wanted to get out to Mexico. We made the attempt, but my wife got sick and couldn't travel. So we had to stay once again in the CPR. We were ninety-six families in that place. Each family was five or six people. We were many. I think it was surprising that so many people were still there.

The army made many plans to see if they could capture all of us. They put various battalions to one side of us. The guerrillas went out to meet them, and they clashed. Instead of capturing [us], the army received their own casualties. The guerrillas attacked them, and didn't let them enter [the communities].

We retreated to the mountains of Mexico. We presented ourselves to immigration in Mexico. They asked where we were going to go. "We have five tons of food for you," they said. "Are you going to Chajul? Or here to Maravillas? Where do you want to go? We will take you right now."

We said, "No, if you want to help us, help us stay some days in these mountains, leave us in peace here. We have food." We had six burros loaded with cane to make sugar. We had a lot of corn to make tortillas. Beans to eat. "If you want to help us, help us stay here. When the Guatemalan Army returns to their base, we will go back to Guatemala."

They [the immigration officials] said they would travel to Mexico City and return in eight days with a decision. If you are here or if you have returned to Guatemala, don't worry. But he took a video of everyone who was there. That is where we encountered the Catholic Church as well. They did not forget us. They came with food, they gave us clothes, medicine, everything we needed—whatever we didn't have.

In eight days, the immigration [officials] returned and said, "We can't let you stay here any longer. If you agree, we will give you an identity [card] from here on the border. But when all that had passed, we returned again to Guatemala. The army had withdrawn, so we went back to the places where we had been. [But they] came after us when they saw that we had returned. Their plan was if they didn't kill us, to drive us out of the area.

In the CPR, we were a long time without food. We planted five hundred cuerdas [about thirty-five acres] of milpa. It was growing well when the army entered and pulled up the corn. Three days later, we planted again. It was a struggle for us. We planted corn; they destroyed it; we planted again. When it was growing ears, they burned it. But they were never able to burn all of it; they left a bit, and we were able to save that. In that way, we were able to survive. At one time, there was no corn for six months. There was a bit from Mexico but very spoiled. And so we began to find a tree that we call jushte . We knew it [by that name], but in a book, I saw it was also called "Ramon, seeds of Ramon." It bears a lot of fruit. We gathered that by the hundreds of pounds. We mixed it with a bit of corn, and we had something to eat. It was good food. During that time, we ate a lot of yucca. Some days, that kept us going until 2 p.m., and other days until evening. [We ate] fruits called *guineo majunche* or *guineo de piña*. They are hard, they don't fall, and the animals don't often eat them because it is not very sweet. When it is very ripe, it is good. All that time that we were there, God helped us with his power, with the things he gave us.

We ate well, even with no corn. Later, we planted again and were able to harvest the corn. We planted vegetables and tomatoes. We planted cabbage, radishes, and watercress, and onions. [We planted] all that by the acre. The corn, it grew so well. We planted, they pulled it up; we planted again, and [the plants] gave corn. We planted it wherever, and it grew. We planted *camote*, we planted yucca, we planted *huisquil*, which in Mexico they call *chayote*.

We had three papaya trees. With three papaya trees, we gave papayas to ninety-six families. They were big ones. Some were ripe when we cut them [down]; we didn't eat them while we were working. We got ten or fifteen each time. It was very organized; we noted the names of the families that had already received one. If it wasn't their turn, it had to go to the others. Then others, then others, like that, until they had been given to the ninety-six families. I remember, at the end there was one papaya tree left, the others had fallen. That was in a sandy place, a beautiful place. And so I say, "Why do you say that God doesn't help [us] when God gives us those things?"

Our son was nine years old. In 1984, on the ninth of February, he was captured by the army. I thought he was dead. They had killed a pig where he was captured, and we didn't know if it was human blood or from an animal. So I thought they had killed him. But later, there were pamphlets thrown from a helicopter saying that we should give ourselves up [to see our son]. But in that time, there were so many lies, we never thought it was true. If we turned ourselves in, they would kill us. For that reason, we had to abandon our son.

Much later, people from the [civil] patrols told me, "No, your son is alive; he is in Huehuetenango." For a long time, he was a nurse, an assistant [at the army base]. He wasn't very old, but he was working there. I investigated after the war but couldn't find out what happened to him.

The pain was terrible. Later, we began to want to leave [the CPR.]. But if we were not there, we would worry about our son. What if he

Baudilio Monzon Martinez and mother's brother, Luis Martinez

came back, and we weren't there. Finally, we decided we had better just stay. If death comes to us, we'll die. Our son was gone, and we may also have to die. So we stayed, but we missed him very much.

Once I went with a group of thirty children to gather vegetables. We were there in the morning when a helicopter showed up and came down in the place, almost where we lived. I said, "Who knows what will happen. Best we pick up our food and move away from where they are so they don't see us." They made a terrible bombardment, but the people were elsewhere. There were ninety-six families. An airplane came and was machine-gunning. It was an A-37. It strafed from one side to another, right where the people were. We thought all the people would be dead. Who knew how many would be killed and how many left alive? When the plane had left, [the children] dropped their cargo and ran to see who had survived. I came behind.

They asked, "Where are the dead?" Not one. That surprised me. I saw that God was protecting us. It didn't touch even a hair on anyone. The bullets dug up the earth, knocked down branches from the trees. But injured? Not even one. "What happened?" The bullets fell there, but they stopped on the surface of the ground . . . how strange. Ninety-six families under [continuous] machine gunning, and not one injured, not even a finger, nothing. Many were out farming their milpa, and the others took shelter in the trenches. "Ah," I said, "the power of God is almighty."

I saw the people were very discontented, very sad. Even though I was not the responsible person, I came forward and told everyone to get out of there, to leave for another known place. The others began to scold me, "Why are you ordering the people around? We don't have 'orders.' Don't command the people." I felt bad for the women; they were very weak. But it was better to go. Padre Ricardo also asked me why I was ordering the people around.

I said, "Father, the A-37 came by very slowly, to see exactly where to shoot. We should leave here so God can continue helping us. Are we going to put God on trial to protect us here? No. If we are out in the open and ask God to protect us, that's not good. He has [already] helped us a lot."

Father saw my point, "You are right. Let's pray, then let's go." That was at four in the afternoon. At five, an official order came that we should all leave. But I had already sent some people, even though I suffered from those who were treating me badly for giving orders. They had treated me poorly, but I . . . .

The plane left. But God also saw us very clearly. Rapidly, the trees filled with clouds. The trees began to move, and drizzle began to fall. We left that day; the next day, it was still closed in with clouds, and the next day. On the third day, it was clear like it is today. The airplane came. It dropped [its bombs] exactly where it had come to shoot. If we had been there, it would have probably killed about five families.

There were twenty-six chickens that belonged to a man who didn't want to take them. He said he'd get them later. He left them closed in there. Those twenty-six ended up in pieces, not one still alive. We saw that the bomb had been a big one.

For me, it was very beautiful that God sees one, even though some say there is no power in God. We get things through our own sweat, our own work. But no, it is something that God watches over us. What we don't see, that is what helps us. He gives us the air, he gives us the water, he gives us the sun. And it all comes to help us. . . .

Dominga Pablo Lucas
María Matías Pablo
Mayalan, June, 11, 2010

María:
Before I was born, I think it was 1964. . .1962 . . . my father, Victoriano Matías Ortiz went down to Ixcán from Todos Santos, but not to the co-operatives. They came to a place called Piedras Blancas, by the hamaca of the Todos Santeros.

Dominga Pablo Lucas and María Matías Pablo

It was they that built it. They came on foot. They arrived at the finca of Bruno Villatoro, but they didn't know that. They thought it was land that didn't have an owner. They began to clear the land, plant their milpa. Don Pablo Mendoza, Don Félix Mendoza, the late Julian Mendoza, and Don Rufino Martín went together with my father, Victoriano, and settled there.

They were there a year, or a bit more, when the *finquero* Bruno Villatoro arrived. He brought all his papers, and showed my father that the land they had settled on was private, that it was his finca.

He gave them a choice. If they wanted to have their milpa, they could clear all the jungle, but without pay. In time, he would plant *zacate*. My father thought, "Why should we continue working since it is for the finquero, and he won't pay anything? Better if I leave." So they returned again to the highlands.

My mother says that I was about to be born. Victoriano came in September, and I was born in October, fifteen days after the Todos Santeros returned. Then they made trips to [work on] the fincas on the south coast.

The idea of the co-operatives had matured within the Diocese of Huehuetenango, so when they went down to Ixcán again, they were better organized. They were accompanied by a priest. [This would have been Maryknoll Father Ed Doheney.] They passed by Padre Guillermo Woods. At that time, he was in Barillas, and so through the coordination of the churches, they came directly to the Primer Centro. There was not the confusion of the first trip. Don Pablo Mendoza, Don Julian Mendoza, Don Felix, and the late Nicolas Mendoza had stayed at the Villatoro finca. When my father returned again, accompanied by the priest, they just moved a little bit farther down to the area of the co-operative. They built their houses more quickly and settled their families. For my father, it was harder. He brought little with him, and then had to go back again to get my mother. When my mother arrived, those three families were already there. She came on my father's third trip. He came alone the first time, with the padre and some other people the second time. Then he returned to get my mother.

Dominga:

We had been on the coast. I was familiar with that. I went to the coast working for a *patrón*. At the hacienda, only potatoes grew. The milpa didn't produce anything.

This place we didn't know. Just "Ixcán." What kind of "*Can*?" [In Mam, Dominga's language, "Ix" means the female, and "Can" means snake. However, the word is not Mam but Kanjobal, with a different meaning.]

In 1964, we came down from Todos Santos, Cuchumatán, Huehuetenango. We arrived at Tres Caminos and contracted some mules to carry our cargo to Barillas. [We went] on a trail on foot. After Barillas, we arrived at San Ramon, then came to the Rio Ixcán. We crossed the Rio Ixcán on a hamaca. It was very narrow. A hamaca that "danced" a lot with the wind. Padre Eduardo came together with us. We arrived on November 7, I think, of 1964,

I was not very happy. We didn't know anything about the place. Here there was no house, nothing, nothing. We came into the jungle. We cleared it. We cut beams to make a shelter. There was nothing to eat, just a plant called *chileta*, sweet *chileta*. It grows wild. That is what we ate for greens. There were some small plants we called *piyaya* in the jungle. My husband gathered it for Maria to eat. We were carrying her. She was this size [indicates a baby]. I was sad when I arrived. We didn't know the area. I was often sick because there were so many flies, mosquitoes . . . . Perhaps like now, but no, now there are many people. When we came down, there were so many insects. We didn't have a mosquito net. We didn't have anything. In our town, there were no mosquitoes. But here, just biting . . . . María was bitten. But where could we go. We didn't have much land in Todos Santos. We came here by necessity because of the poverty of the land. When we came down here, we came for once and for all.

For a long time, we lived in a small house, just a shelter. We had little medicine. They made an airstrip in the First Center, and Padre Eduardo brought his plane from Guatemala City. He brought medicine, and then he built a clinic. It was small, just a thatch hut. Later, when some time had passed, we planted milpa, beans, everything. We planted pumpkin and tomatoes. But [that was] much later. It was a struggle.

Padre Eduardo was together with us in the shelter. The house just had stalks of wild cane for walls. Then we began to work. Some-one from Santa Eulalia came to cut boards. It wasn't like now, one person can cut with a chainsaw. Before, there had to be two people. They had to build a sawpit, then put the log on top. One person was above and one below, and the saw passed between them. Then they made a plank house for Padre Eduardo.

María:

Now, I can involve myself a bit more politically. I didn't have much education before. They didn't send me to school. My mother says they were in the jungle, and she was afraid. My father was gone a lot to the capital, to Huehuetenango, to the diocese. He had to leave my mother alone. My brothers went to study, but she kept me for company.

Dominga:

Only the oldest was in school, Jorge was young . . . . I was alone. [María] was young also. I was afraid of the jaguars. The Cerro Cuache was full of jaguars. Victoriano brought a dog who would sleep inside so the jaguars wouldn't take him. The jaguars didn't bother us. No, they just took the chickens. There is a kind they call *tigrillo*. That is what was taking them . . . . They visited me but only took my chickens. Before, there were many chickens. They didn't have sicknesses, nothing. Not like now.

Victoriano was named as a leader. All the people coming down passed through my husband. He helped make the contract so they could get their parcela. He asked if they were good people, if they had committed an offense in their hometowns.

Padre Eduardo said, "If a bad person from their pueblo wants to come here to get land, he better not. I don't want to give the land to just any kind of person, someone who doesn't have good charac-ter. In the beginning, if it was a single man or single woman, they couldn't get a parcela. If they were married, had a wife, had a hus-band, they got the parcela.

David came, he was an engineer. He surveyed and gave out the parcelas.

María:

Victoriano worked in the clinic, and he cooked in the padre's kitchen. He went back and forth between the clinic and the kitchen. He went to help unload the plane. He visited the people. He did a lot of work. He had experience in resolving many problems that the co-operative had with boundaries. There was a problem in Mónaco, another in Ixtuacán Chiquito, with the boundaries of the co-operative. He was capable of helping to resolve these problems. There was also a problem with the Second Center. That group wanted to be independent of the co-operative, but they were within the land of the co-operatives. They looked for a solution, an alternative to try to resolve this problem.

We were content when there was milpa. We had pigs. The years we were here, we were happy.

José (Chepe) Sales Ramirez
Mayalan, February 18, 2011 and November 20, 2012

Originally, I was from Ixtuacán San Ildefonso, Huehuete-nango. I speak Mam. My name is José Sales Ramirez. I was thirty-four years old when I came down here. But here, I got old. [laughs] I turned seventy-four last March.

I was working on the south coast, renting land. I worked in the coffee and cotton plantations. Life was very hard. Sometimes, the owners didn't pay us. We were all tired. But to make a move with a whole family was very hard. We had to make arrangement . . . . For us, it was far. And there was no road. I made an agreement with my wife. For the love of the earth, I would go down to Ixcán to see. I came for the first time in 1966, when Padre Eduardo entered [with] the Todos Santos campesinos, and later those from other pueblos. The land was beautiful. I met Victoriano Matías Ortíz and other companions. It was nice. They talked about it being a co-operative, a place for the poor people.

But there was no way to bring things in, like food, like salt and sugar. And so the people began to work on an airstrip in the First Center. I worked there for fifteen days. There were no parcelas. They were beginning to survey the land. There was an engineer named Roberto Rothman. They were cutting survey lines from the First to the Fourth Center.

I learned what the conditions were to be able to join the co-operative. And then I went back to make my plans. [That was] 1966.

It took four years to prepare. I came down with all my family in 1970. I don't mean to say that my pueblo was no good. I felt bad to leave, but there was no land there. The majority of us came to Ixcán from different municipalities, from different departments. Many poor came. When the co-operative first began, it was very beautiful. Everything was lively . . . .

We came on foot. I'll tell you, it was something else. When we arrived at Huehuetenango, I said to my wife, "Let's get rubber boots." The women were not accustomed [to wearing them]. They didn't want to wear boots. They looked ugly. But I said, "Wife, it's not for you to like them but so that we can walk. If you don't want to come with me, stay here. I'm going with my children, with those who can walk."

My wife said, "How could you leave me?"

"Well, if you don't want to go . . . ."

"And when you get there, what will you do? For sure, you will take another woman." There was a fight, a disagreement.

"For sure," I said, "because I will need a woman. There, they won't give a parcela to a single person, only to a couple. So if you don't want [to go], I won't force you."

My wife began to cry. "How can I stay here?"

"Let's go then. If you agree, put on your boots. Let's walk. I know the way."

"How many days will it take to get there?"

We went by bus to Barillas. "In Barillas, we can buy your boots." We arrived with four families. ¡Ay! Dios, the poor other women. Their men had not told them to buy boots. So on the path, they began to argue with the women and got mad. They wanted to return in mid-journey. Well, it was hard, but we had reached an agreement. There was nothing more to say. We left Barillas at two in the afternoon and walked the rest of the day. We were carrying the children; we had four. We walked about five kilometers, stopped and left [again] at dawn. My daughter, who is now in the capital, was riding on my pack. She was happy, singing. My wife put on her boots. She was willing. We walked another day, all day, and came to a place called Río Espíritu. There we slept.

José (Chepe) Sales Ramirez

My brother-in-law also came. He brought two boys. He carried them in a big box, the two boys and the food for the journey. But the lasso that went around the box was chaffing. We crossed the Río Espíritu around eight in the morning. The lasso parted. The boys and the box fell in. What chaos! The mother was furious with her husband because the children were bruised.

There were conditions for the entry of a person [into the co-operative]: that he be a hard-working person, that he get along, [things] like that. I liked it a lot. A new [arrival] had to cut down twenty cuerdas [almost an acre and a half] of jungle for a sponsor. I did that and more. I did thirty cuerdas, because I liked to work. There were many fears of the wild animals, that they might do something, that they would attack someone. The jaguars were big animals. In Mayalan, many of us came to build an airstrip. At three or four in the morning, on the other side of the clearing, the jaguars were growling. They made a sound like a burro. It strikes fear, but they did no harm.

Then came the time of Padre Guillermo Woods. Padre Woods expanded the work. But the engineers didn't really want to work; things didn't advance. So Padre Guillermo made a plan to take the younger men, the sons of co-op members, to Guatemala City for training as surveyors, guided by David. Then things moved forward. David coordinated the work. He was a valiant man. I miss him. May he rest in peace.

I got my parcela in 1971. I went to Xalbal. All was good. It was very lively. The only thing was, it was hard to walk in the mud, and it was hard to open the pathways. I met various paisanos of Guatemala, from Todos Santos, Santa Eulalia, and San Sebastian, Santa Barbara. The poor came down here from all those municipalities to look for land.

Padre Guillermo organized many things in the co-operative. The first step he took was to organize the health aides and education. He petitioned for teachers, gave an incentive for teachers from the co-operative itself. I liked all this movement.

The only way to bring things in was with Padre Guillermo's airplane. The airstrip at the First Center was where cargo arrived, later here in Mayalan, and still later in Xalbal. In 1971, when I came to Xalbal, the airstrip was not finished, so we worked there. That was where I got to know David the most. It was a big job. There was a chain saw to cut up all the big logs that were scattered on the airstrip. We cleaned it up, dug out the tree stumps. It was a lot of work. Padre Giullermo took a five-pound ax and cut the big logs. There was a chain saw over there, other people here, others burning the branches . . . . That is how it was done.

We had permission from Civil Aviation. With the help of lawyers, the padre, and the directors of the co-operative, all the airstrips were legalized.

When you speak of a co-operative, I like that word very much because of the meaning of "co-operative." To do a job together, to build bridges over the arroyos, to haul logs of fifteen, twenty meters—for here there are big logs—all without being forced. The people did the *mano de obra*. It took two hundred or two hundred fifty people to haul a log. Since there were no ropes, they just used vines, big vines that the people wrapped around their waist. The log moved like a snake, everyone pulling. Well, with many people, you can do anything. They also made hamacas over [arroyos] . . . . The best was the hamaca over the Rio Ixcán. I liked the co-operative because we united our forces and did everything.

When I was in my pueblo, I was already taking courses [to be a] health aide. I trained here in Ixcán, then I went to Jacaltenango to finish with Doctor Juana [Jane Buellesbach, a Maryknoll Sister]. I worked as an aide in Xalbal, where we built a clinic.

There weren't [many] people, so they gave me a double workload. I sold things in the co-op store, and I managed the selling of medicines in the clinic. I could take out molars, give injections, intramuscular and intravenous. All that. Those skills helped a lot. In 1971–1972, I was president of the co-operative in Xalbal. 1973 and 1974 were good years. We were planting products like coffee and cardamom. In three years, we were harvesting. A group of us joined together in a center called Centro la Palmera, where I lived. We were just fourteen families, but we incorporated as members. We worked together. We worked one day with one family, another day with another, like that.

We made a contract among all of us to buy a coffee roaster. All the fourteen families made an agreement to plant ten cuerdas [about three-quarters of an acre] each. Oh, it was so nice. In three years, it was giving the first harvest. In four years, we had coffee to sell, [and] cardamom. Many things were changing. We had arrived at first without money. We continued solving problems, improving our lives. We had a place to work, to plant milpa. Here, the land was good, very good, very productive. Everything grew. Back then, I was strong. I planted pineapple and yucca. Fruit trees, orange, *nance*, everything.

In the year 1975, the bad times began. When the internal war started, we didn't understand. But at this time, we saw that they were prohibiting the small planes of Padre [from flying]. The army came, establishing military bases. They began on the other side of the river, in Santiago Ixcán, in Kaibil Balam. They also came to Xalbal and built a military fort. And what did they say? They said, "We are putting the military here to guard all the campesinos." But we wondered why. What for? We had been [here] for a long time, living with many wild animals which were dangerous but never caused us harm.

The kidnapping began, and so started the fear in all the members of the co-op. Life was not good. There was a lot of control. I remember the tenth of June. It was a Sunday. Nine people were kidnapped. I didn't understand why. Three helicopters landed. Many soldiers came and surrounded the town. The people were not worried. It was market day. They had herbs, bananas, chickens for sale, pigs for sale. I observed each person brought something different to the market. The people were good. When the army arrived, we were very surprised.

They took nine persons. They took a health aide named Miguel Sales Ordoñez, my first cousin. The others, I don't remember [all] their names—one was named Sebastian Felipe, Alonso Ortiz, Gabriel Matías, Ah, there is more—I don't remember; they were members [of the co-op]. They took them away in a helicopter. Even now, we still don't know their whereabouts.

At two in the afternoon, the army came into the co-op store where I was. There was no one [but me]. Everyone had gone. I couldn't go out because they had the whole town surrounded. They came inside to check everything that was in there. They beat me but they left me alive. I was able to make it to my house. Many orphans were left, many widows. That is something I wanted to say. . . . I don't think I will forget them, especially the smallest children.

One was afraid to walk from one center to another. We had to walk with our documents. If they asked for them and we didn't have them, they beat us or tortured us. The kidnapping that was happening, for example, in Xalbal also occurred here in Mayalan, in Cuarto Pueblo, everywhere that is within the area of Ixcán Grande. Because of the presence of the army, there was a lot of control, threats, and false accusations. The people were alarmed. There was a demonstration; all the community was present. "What do we do? And where to file a complaint?" A delegation went to the capital to denounce [what had happened], but the authorities paid no attention. Many companions and I were there, demonstrating on behalf of my first cousin and other friends who were kidnapped, asking why they were captured? What had they done? We visited the offices of the authorities. We left letters with the government, the ministry of defense, describing everything that was happening in the area of Ixcán. But the next day, they announced that what we reported was not true. They said, "It could be that the persons disappeared because of the guerrillas."

We were [all] in this same situation, not just because of the abductions. I spoke of the kidnapping, but the army had done more. [They destroyed] the houses in the communities. They killed the pigs and turkeys if they went out on the street. They said they were jungle animals. We withstood much, much. All the people wanted to speak [out]. Those who spoke the most, the kidnapping began [with them]. Whoever spoke out, the next week, they weren't there.

We couldn't speak with a strong enough voice as only [the people of] Xalbal, Pueblo Nuevo, Mayalan, the five co-operatives. There had been other abductions in Santa Maria Tzeja. In Santiago Ixcán, the president of the co-operative, named Diego Toma, had been abducted. In San Jose la Venta, our companion Randolfo was kidnapped, and another named Domingo Quichan. A teacher was abducted in Mayalan, the same in Cuarto Pueblo. They were our friends. We knew them all.

Representatives from those communities got together. We talked about what was happening in the co-operative of Ixcán Grande. We united to denounce it, but the notice was never published during the time of President Lucas Garcia. They censored all the radio stations, the newspapers. They also assassinated journalists. At that time, everything remained in obscurity. There was no news, We couldn't protest. And so the decision was taken to talk to an embassy. Here, there was an audience who would receive these declarations about what was happening in Guatemala. The first to organize were the five co-operatives of Ixcán Grande. Later, there was coordination with other communities beyond the Rio Xalbal, including the co-operatives of the Zona Reina. There was a meeting with all the representatives of the communities in the area of Ixcán. From Mayalan went Chus Camposeco, Chico Carillo, and Manuel Ross. From Pueblo Nuevo, Jesús Figueroa and Mateo Silvestre. From Quiche, Vicente Menchu. He was in an organization of the unions of Guatemala. They also had families here in Ixcán at Santa Maria Tzeja, where there were a lot of kidnappings. And so we all united, we campesinos, the workers, the poor.

A date was named for taking over the embassy. It was in January 1981. The first groups arrived, among them the father of Rigoberta Menchu. We were about to arrive, but it wasn't yet our time to die. The car broke down on the road. We waited until the car was fixed, and then we went on to the embassy. But we couldn't get to it. The control was [already in place] about two blocks away. No one could enter. Later, the news came out that the Spanish Embassy had been burned. It was painful. The people were burned up, the whole site of the Spanish embassy. It is sad to remember that. I think about thirty-seven people were killed. We went to the wake for the victims.

There is a saying that we shouldn't talk about the past, but it isn't so. We have to tell our story because it wasn't easy; it was hard. Many people died, hundreds of people, children and the elderly. That was the year 1975. In 1976, incrementally more things happened. There was more control; one couldn't move about. Life was bad. In the fields and farms, one could see the soldiers, the soldiers going out, searching the jungle. What we didn't understand was "Why?" They never told us. We thought that it was because the land in Ixcán was like a young woman. We thought, that's it; they want to take the land because the majority of us were poor . . . the anger of the rich. . . . I say this because I think that at one time, the owners of the fincas were left without workers and that this was the [reason for] their anger. Maybe they felt the blow, because the finca owners only lived by the sweat of the poor. When so many came down here to Ixcán, there were fewer workers in the fincas, the cane fields, the cotton fields. We were thinking that perhaps [the violence was] due to that.

Thanks be to God, Padre Guillermo, in peace may he rest, fought to get land titles in the names of the five co-operatives. If he hadn't done that, then probably we couldn't have recovered this land. He made this sacrifice. But sadly, they killed him on the twentieth of November of 1976. First, those campesinos were kidnapped, then they killed the padre. It put fear into all the people

I think they killed him, because his plane crashed in San Juan Coatzal [near an army base]. That was a great sadness for all the people, many people crying, children, the women. Every time Padre came . . . he was always smiling. Sitting with the children in the fields. . . . That was a great pain, and we will never forget. . . . Thanks be to God, we have his body; he didn't die, he is here with us. It is something.

After all that happened in 1976, 1977, '78 . . . . In 1980, my God, we couldn't go on. They began to burn the houses. That is when they killed many people. So what was there now for us? Those of us who could, left. Those who couldn't, stayed . . . dead. There are so many unburied bones scattered here in the jungle.

We had to flee, but there was nowhere to go. We thought the best was to go to Mexico. One afternoon on the twentieth of June of 1980, there was a bombardment in Cerro Cuache and in the town. Huge bombs fell. But thanks to God, not one person died. Only one dog, they say, was killed on the airstrip. This began at 6:30 in the evening. They didn't stop machine gunning until eight at night. All the people were afraid. It was night. It was like lightning, the lights of the machine guns from above, the bombs . . . . But the next day, the army went to the houses saying, "What happened to you? No one was injured? No one?"

"No," we said, "no."

"Maybe there was. Let us see inside. Don't try to hide them; we are going to kill them." They looked, but there were no dead persons. Just the dog died, and the trees where the bombs fell. God is great; no one was injured. But it was a frightening thing.

After that, we finally decided to go to Mexico. But it was difficult. To cross the border with my family took fourteen days. It is not far; normally, it only took one day to get there. But when we left, we heard the army shooting up ahead, so we had to backtrack, and go through the pure jungle. For that, our machetes were useful, to open a path. We went in circles getting to Mexico.

It isn't easy to [be refugees]; there was a lot of suffering. We arrived in a place called Puerto Rico, close to the border on the bank of the Rio Ixcán Grande. A Mexican who lived there was named Antonio Sanchez. I think now he is dead. Thanks to that man. . . . He didn't turn us away. He received all of us poor people. But many of the children and the elderly died. The leaders asked for a place to bury them, a cemetery. That man gave ten cuerdas [about three-quarters of an acre] of land for a cemetery. Quickly, we filled one cuerda, in a year. How many children? Malnourished, from hunger . . . old people, they died. So many dead in that place.

I can't say that we were free. Often, there were incursions by the Guatemalan army. Now, the Mexicans understood that the armies of Guatemala were not good people. Guatemalan soldiers killed two

Mexicans, thinking they were Guatemalans. That is when the Mexicans reacted strongly. Then they paid attention to us.

In the year 1984, people were sent to Quintana Roo, to Campeche. It was not so easy. The people didn't want to go, but the Mexican commission forced us to. "You are going to die here; they have killed two Mexican families. There is no security for you here. It is better to go far away."

Each person was wondering [what to do]. I thought we should go. So we went to Quintana Roo. Others went to Campeche. It was very hard. We were packed together in a building like chickens on a farm. Well, we were fleeing from the army, so . . . . We asked for something to plant, because most of us who fled were campesinos. We needed to work the land so we could eat. But in Mexico, there were problems with the [local] campesinos. Now, we foreigners were asking to be given a piece of land. No! We were ten years there, suffering very much. So we began to think of returning [to Ixcán] where we had land.

It took a long time. Negotiations began, and there was a meeting called Esquipulas II, consisting of the five presidents of Central America. They were to analyze what could be done about the war. Members of international human rights groups were there. They demanded [answers from] the government: "What do you think about the refugees?" I remember this man—I don't know if he is still alive—from the international human rights, named Christian Tomoscha. He asked, "What plan do you have for the refugees, for their return?"

Vinicio Cerezo Arévalo [the newly elected Guatemalan president] said, "That is not a problem because there are no refugees. All the Guatemalans have returned because they heard that [there is] a civilian president, me. And so there is not one Guatemalan outside of the borders of their country." But it was all a lie. We in Mexico saw that the Guatemalan government didn't take us into account. They said there was no delegation representing us. And so in 1987, the people began to organize the Permanent Commissions.

In the year 1988, the Permanent Commissions were formed. [Members] were elected. And as a national dialogue had been opened, the commissions began to petition to participate in this dialogue. They sent many letters, but the government of Vinicio Cerezo never answered. He turned a deaf ear on us.

At the CNR, the National Committee of Reconciliation, there was a bishop who the government itself named during the assembly of Esquipulas II. He was Monsignor Rodolfo Quezada Toruño, the mediator for the government. Maybe they thought they could take advantage of him, but [because of] the monsignor, we were accepted. And so the Permanent Commissions were present at the national dialogue.

The Guatemalans in Mexico rose up. They took a census of all the people in Mexico, in Quintana [Roo], in Campeche, in the Valley of Mexico. The result was that there were forty-eight thousand Guatemaltecos in Mexico. Vinicio Cerezo didn't want to accept [these results] because he thought the Permanent Commission was self-appointed. But no, they were elected in a general assembly of all the sectors. Even the governor of the state was present, [as well as] a delegation from immigration. They were witnesses.

Vinicio Cerezo left [the presidency]. Now, it was Jorge Serrano Elias. He signed the return agreement but only after a long struggle. Our efforts were united with those of all the organizations in Guatemala. They helped us, as Guatemalans, as poor who were demanding a return with certain conditions. The government did not want that. But thanks be to God, thanks to all the work and struggle, an agreement for the return was signed on the eighth of October 1992.

In Quintana Roo, there were eight thousand and some refugees. In the assembly there, I was elected as a representative to the National Dialogue. My substitute was the late Juan Cok, may he rest in peace. We accepted the wishes of the people. You can't say that I did it. It was done by the Permanent Committees, with the backing of the people.

In Mexico, ACNUR, the United Nations High Commission for Refugees, took care of all the poor refugees, helping us with food, medicine. When a large group of people organizes, it [carries] a lot of weight. All the forty-eight thousand refugees in Mexico united through the Permanent Commissions. There were also many international institutions, like the churches, who helped us. They accompanied us. We had a finance committee which arranged for the transportation. The refugees themselves also helped.

I couldn't get back my original parcela in the Ixcán. It is sad to remember that. I had my parcela in Xalbal, but now, I am here in Mayalan. Why? Not because I wanted it. When we returned in the year 1993, our return was to a crossroads. We thought we would return to our parcelas. For two years, we lived on the side of the road in Veracruz. We arrived the ninth of December of 1993. There was a lot of negotiation about reentering Xalbal. We were two hundred fifty-six parcelistas from Xalbal; I think half had arrived.

Even though we returned while [the land] was [still] abandoned, others had gotten legal papers [land titles] for the area from Xalbal to Primer Centro. According to the explanation given by the army, a region had to be given to the ex-[civil] patrollers, the refugees would [get] a different piece, and the CPR [another]. There would be one region for the refugees, one for the CPR, and one for the soldiers. Those were the plans we saw. But this didn't happen.

The land title was originally in the name of the co-op, but they took advantage to make individual titles. It was sad to see that. I didn't like it, but what could be done? I waited two years until finally we saw that we couldn't [get our land]. It is not to say my parcela was invalidated, but they made an exchange. They took advantage. They left the land that was not too good, and in Xalbal, they took the good fertile land. My parcela was all bottomland. I received [another] here in Center 11. It is not the same; it is very broken. But there we are. Now I am here in Mayalan.

And the other half, those unfortunates who returned without preconditions, I think they suffered more. Their morale was crushed by the army.

When there is a fiesta in Xalbal, and I say to my wife, "Let's go to the fiesta," she doesn't want to.

"If I go there, I am going to cry," she says. There has been a lot of suffering, but thanks be to God, here we are.

Facunda Monzón Matias
Mayalan, June 10, 2010

My name is Facunda Monzón Matias. I was born in San Pedro Necta, Department of Huehuetenango.

My father came to Ixcán to see the land. He was struck to see a land so rich that everything grew. When he returned to our pueblo, he began to say to my mother that he wanted to go to Ixcán because there was good land. Everything grew. You didn't need fertilizer. You just planted, and everything grew. There in the highlands, it was more temperate. You had to add fertilizer. You had to struggle with the land. It was very difficult work.

He decided to go, but my mother . . . well . . . as we had a piece of land in San Pedro ... it was very small, but she felt we were fine with the land we had. Ultimately, my father said, "I'm going. If you want to go, let's go. If not, stay here." My mother had given birth to my little sister just two months earlier. Then my father said to the children, "Who wants to go with me to Ixcán? I'm going." Some of my brothers were older. [When my father told them how it was], they became enthusiastic, and said, "I'm going with my papa." "I'm going," said another. "I'm going," said another. Three were going. We, the younger ones, didn't give an answer but finally said we would go. At night, my mother began to cry and cry. "What am I going to do? Better to go." We began to pack our things.

And so we came. I was four years old, but I still remember. My mother said, "Let's go, daughter. " I didn't want to go. I wanted to stay there with her. We packed the cargo and went on a bus to Huehuetenango and Barillas. We were in Barillas for eight days. There weren't big buildings, just small huts. After eight days, my father said. "Let's go. We have to get to Ixcán." We thought Barillas was the place where we were going to stay. He said, "No, we're not there yet."

But from Barillas to Mayalan, there was no bus. The trucks only went [as far as] Tres Ranchos, no more. We stopped there. "From here, we have to go on foot." I still barely remember. My father walked in front carrying a big load.

My two uncles, Modesto and Ángel Alvarado, were [in Ixcán]. [We met] the late Juan Alvarado and Gaspar Alvarado and Don Pedro. They lived here [in Mayalan] on the hill. We went along the path. "We will get to where your uncles are," they said. We got to San Ramón and were there for three days. I remember that there were some houses . . . that there was cheese. I remember the cheese. We were sitting there on the edge of the path with my brothers and sisters. We got the cheese, divided it, and began to eat.

There were some leaves of *kekeste grande,* and something we called *capote.* We cooked and ate it there in San Ramón. From there, we continued the walk. In places, my father was cutting a path. Because he had a load [on his back], it was hard to pass in the jungle. He cut the path [with a machete], clearing it until he could pass. It took two days to get to Primer Centro. We came with all the family, walking . . . . When night came, we stopped . . . . When we arrived, we were all crying because my father had told us there would be a bus to where we were going. He completely tricked us into coming.

We met Victoriano. We stayed in Primer Centro eight days. Then we came here to Mayalan. It was the same walking to Mayalan. There was a tiny path. Since my father had a load, it was difficult. There were mosquitoes and the jaguars. They came close to the house. The jaguars hunted the dogs, hunted the chickens. And my mother, crying. She cried in hopelessness. But my father had made a decision. And so, for the love of the land, he brought us to Ixcán. It was good land.

Little by little, we went on, afraid of the jaguars, afraid of the animals, wild pigs, deer, afraid of everything. At that time, all was si-

Facunda Monzón Matias

lence. The jungle was virgin. No one went [there]. Everything, the snakes, everything was watching. But, little by little, we grew accustomed, but my mother cried. She would cry [in front of] us. [We had been convinced] that where we were going to live, there would be machines, that we could go in buses. [We] asked, "Are there cars there, papa?" "Yes," he said. "There are . . . ." He convinced us. When we got here, there were no cars, just jaguars and wild pigs.

We began to farm, to plant, to harvest the fruits, the corn, beans, everything that grew. My father began to build. I think, Miguel, you still remember that he worked with Don David when they began to build the runways. He worked on the runways for the five co-operatives. He was content because he was working, and because the harvest of corn and beans had begun. On the other hand, in the highlands it had been very difficult. Finally, he sold the land in the highlands to ensure that we wouldn't go back. And since we didn't have a place to go back to, we continued coping.

That is how we arrived in Ixcán. That is what I remember.

When the repression began complicating things, that was another problem. [We had] to leave the land here and go into the jungle because of the repression by the army. During the times of the violence, we were [in the CPR] for fourteen years.

My father . . . . Well, it was like this. When we were here, he was very content. He worked; he had his things. He planted sufficient cane, bananas, beans, corn, and he bought a mill to grind cane. Before the repression, we had a big shed where he ground the cane. He made *panela* [a form of unrefined sugar]. He sold panela and honey.

When the violence began, both sides, the guerrillas and army, began to kill. They killed one, killed another. That's how it began. The [army] kidnapped people. We were afraid to sleep in the houses. My father said, "It is bad here. In the evening, we will go sleep in the jungle." All the family had been sleeping in the jungle for eight days [when] we heard the army coming. They were burning the people in the Fourth Center. We saw billows of smoke. They were burning the houses. The parcela there was on a high hill, and we could see the smoke on Cerro Cuache. My father's goddaughter came running. She lived in the Fourth Center. She said, "They are burning the Fourth Center. They are burning all the houses." We escaped. But they had already burned the houses. She was crying. "I couldn't save anything." During the day, we stayed in the house, but we put out guards. All of us from Center Eleven and Center Twenty joined together in my father's house out at his parcela. The people from Center Eleven stayed under the shed for the mill. Those from Center Twenty made shelters in a flat spot to one side. Others had some nylon sheeting. During the day, we cooked in the house. There, we learned, little by little, to cook collectively, together, for everyone, in one pot. In the day, we could keep watch, hear where they were, from where they were coming. But at night, we would go to sleep in the jungle.

At the time, I just had two children, my son Vidal and my daughter who died in the jungle. We had hung our beds under the trees [and] were sleeping when one day, a notice arrived. We could return because the army was far away. They are not patrolling now. We returned to sleep in the houses. The grown sons of the people of Centers Eleven and Twenty were the ones who were on guard. They put one guard here at the Rio Pescado, another at the entrance from B-8, another by the Fourth Center, another at the First Center. If they sent a notice that there was nothing happening, we could sleep peacefully. But when the army was on the move, we didn't stay in the houses. Then it got worse. We couldn't be in the houses during the day. So we all decided to leave. I don't know how they coordinated everyone. We went to Centro Estrellita.

The army attacked us at the Rio Pescado. They were flying over us. We walked a little bit, hid in the jungle, walked a bit more, hid in the jungle. When they were flying over us, we didn't move. When we got to Estrellita, they were flying over us. We didn't light any fires because they were searching for us.

Those in Centro Estrellita were organized. Ana María was there, Doña Ana María, her brother Sebastian Hernández. All of them were there. When we arrived, they received us with food, with atole.

We began to work together. People co-operated to gather corn and beans. We cooked in one [pot]. At first, there was one corn grinder, and we were many families. We took turns grinding. We took turns getting water, gathering leaves for making tamales.

Of course, it was not the same as one person cooking by herself, to her own taste. Now, if the beans burned, the beans burned; if the beans were acidic, they were acidic. But we ate them.

In 1982, my father was with us. The repression got worse. We walked from place to place. The army followed us. When there was an emergency, we all gathered to go to another camp. We changed from one camp to another, and another. We continued like that, but the army persecuted us more. We couldn't live in the jungle. They came after us daily. We couldn't cook. There were more and more people. Because we were so many, we weren't able to grind enough corn through the night. We were thirty families. We couldn't be such a large group, so, little by little, we divided up into groups of ten families. My uncle Angel, my uncle Alfonso, and two [other] men were the leaders. They found two more corn grinders. Then we could [share], ten [families] on each grinder. It helped us to make enough food for the children.

The children couldn't live freely. They had to keep quiet. One looked for a rag and tied it over their mouths so they wouldn't cry out [when] the army was chasing us. At that time, the life in the CPR was very difficult. I still remember a time when the army was close by. A mother put a towel over the mouth of her child so he wouldn't cry. She tied it like this, and the boy couldn't breathe. The señora in charge cried out to her and pulled her hand off. When she let go, the boy [was] about to die.

[When] the army went away, the children were free but not so free that they could cry out. One had to be watching them so they didn't cry, and that they didn't go out to play, in order that the army wouldn't hear them.

At that time, my father was still around. When the army withdrew we, more or less, were free to work, although with lookouts posted. They planted milpa. There were plots of eighty, a hundred fifty cuerdas [five and a half acres, ten and a half acres]. They planted together, harvested together.

But in the time of more repression, when the army launched its offensives, the army cut down the milpa with machetes. If the corn had ears when they cut it down, it was completely lost. [The men of the CPR] went to plant again. At times, they were able to harvest it, at times no. When they could harvest, they filled big bins, and there was corn to eat. But if the army found the bins, they set them on fire.

When that happened, we ate the fruit of the jushte tree and papaya roots. The center of the stalk is soft. We peeled it green. It was chopped fine, and we ground it. We added a bit of maiz, jushte, and green bananas. We called it *"hunche."* You grind it to make tamales when there is no corn. We gave it to the children, but it was not enough to fill them. It was rationed. There would be just two tamales for each one, no more. Even if the child cried that he wanted more, there was none.

My father went to look for taro root or yucca. Everyone went, and what they brought back was rationed. There would be one taro, one yucca for each one. And if there wasn't enough, we cooked just a small piece per person.

The life in the CPR was very sad and painful. To remember, it still pains me. Everyone suffered. We would leave in a rush if the army was coming. We went out at night, at one in the morning, at two in the morning. We left running, carrying what we could. What remained behind remained. After the army passed through, we returned to look for our things.

Finally, the moment came when we couldn't live in the jungle anymore. People began to make plans to get out, to live in Mexico in exile. The notice arrived, and they asked us what we would do, if we would leave. "No," [my father] said. "I'm not going. If you want to go, go on, but I'm not leaving. I'm staying here. I have to recover my parcela. I'm going to plant my cane; I'm going to continue my work. I don't know how I'll do it, but I'm not going. I'm not going to give my sweat, my strength to the Mexicans. I'm not going." And so we didn't move. Time went by, the army chasing us. He didn't regret the suffering. He said, "I'm going to continue resisting here."

When the first ones left, my mother said, "Let's go. It's better if we leave [even if] your father doesn't want to." But we never went into exile. He said, "I'll never go into exile. I'm going to fight for my land. I have to see the end. I have to recover my parcela. I'm not going to Mexico. You, old lady, if you want to, you go," he said to my mother. "Go. Take your children. I'm not going. I'm going to get back my parcela. Since he never left, my mother didn't go either. And so we stayed.

Then the army launched an offensive. At that time, we were in a camp that didn't have a [separate] exit. It was broken country. The entry and exit were together, with a path down below in a low spot, and the entry above, on a ridge. The army came in through the entry from a *barranco* [ravine]. To escape, we left through the exit below. But they opened fire. My father had gone to hide some things. He was on the same path where the lookout was. But the lookout wasn't alert, wasn't watching. Some said he had disassembled his rifle and was cleaning it. It wasn't the moment to not be alert. The watchman should have made a signal if the army was coming. He should have fired, but he didn't.

They entered the camp where we were. They shot my father. It hit him in the mouth and came out in the in the back of his neck. It didn't kill him and he ran. They caught him and cut off both his ears, cut off his hands and his feet, and his head. He carried a small machete in his belt. They left him turned over, took the machete from his scabbard, and inserted it in his back. They left him there, dead. When they killed my father, we couldn't return to get anything. It was 1983 when he died. We were left alone.

My brothers made the decision to stay. There wasn't anyone to argue with them. [But] my mother said, "No." As I was seven months' pregnant with my daughter Jenifer, I couldn't run during the emergencies. We decided to go. I think it was eight months after they killed [my father]. It was difficult to be without him, and the sadness exhausted us more and more.

I said to my husband, "I'm going to go." "No," he said, "I'm not going. I have to fight for the blood of my father-in-law. I'm not going." And my brothers said the same. "We will fight for the blood of our father. He stayed here, and here we will see how it ends, if we recover our land or not."

But the army offensive grew more intense. I said to my uncle and my husband, Bruno, "I'm going because I can't endure it. Let's go, have the baby, and if the situation isn't good, we'll return again." And so I left to give birth to my daughter in Puerto Rico [in Mexico].

We stayed in Puerto Rico for one year and eleven months. But we weren't "declared." We weren't out in the open, just hidden there in the house. Then we returned [to the Ixcán]. But we had to go to Puerto Rico again with all the people to escape the army. Then finally we went back into the jungle again, into the resistance. My mother returned with us. Only my father wasn't there. We were there for fourteen years, with a lot of suffering. In places, there was [no] water. We arrived in a camp. The children wanted water, food, but there was none. [Men] left to look for water. They returned. "There is no water, my friends; there's no water." We passed the night without drinking or eating. In the morning, they looked again. Finally, they found one small jar of dirty water for each one. It looked like mud. We rationed a little bit for each one. We kept on walking looking for water far from the army camp. When we were near a river, there was sufficient. When we were where there was no water, we suffered.

It began to get a bit better when aid entered from Mexico. The sisters and brothers of the Catholic Church of Mexico helped us. The Sisters from Poza Rica, from Maravilla, Tinejapa, other Sisters from Comalapa helped us. We got some sugar, a little milk, salt, soap. If even a tiny bit, it helped us. Our clothes were worn out; everything was patched. We didn't have shoes; we didn't have clothes. We didn't have anything. But then we heard we could more or less go and work in Mexico, even though we were illegal. So at one time, my husband thought, "We don't have any change of [clothes].

"I'm going to Mexico," he said.

I said, "No, I have three children. What will I do there with three children?"

"I'm going," he said. "I'm going to work and buy each one a pair of boots, one change of clothes each, one jacket, and a corn grinder."

Eight days after he left, what they called the counter-offensive began. The offensives had been bearable, but now, the army redoubled its offensives. They patrolled all around, by day and by night. Six months of counter-offensive. We couldn't stay in one camp. When it was "normal," we were in camps for fifteen days, twenty days, one month, two months, like that. But in those six months, we had to move six times, up to ten times a day, moving all the day. It was hard. There was a man who cooked separately but ate with us. He was the one [who carried] my cargo. He helped me.

[My husband] went to Mexico but couldn't make anything. He was in Flor de Café. He could hear the helicopters, the bombardments. He was worried. "What's happening to my family?" When he returned, he only brought a cooking pot and a pair of boots for the children. "I couldn't get anything for you. I heard the bombardment, heavier each time. So I came back. I couldn't make enough."

"Okay," I said, "[we'll get by] with what you brought."

Little by little, things calmed down. After six months, the army left us alone; they withdrew to their bases. Once in a while, they sent a patrol from Pueblo Nuevo. They fired [artillery] from Ixtuacán and Xalbal. But they left us [relatively] free. In one camp, we stayed three months. In another, we stayed about five months. We felt more or less safe.

The dancing didn't stop. Every eight days, there was a dance. Every eight days, there was a marimba. The marimba players were from my family. Two brothers, Reyes Monzón and Juan Monzón, my nephew, the nephew of my husband, Selso Gomez. He is here in Mayalan. And Gonzalo, my godfather. They are in Los Angeles. And another who went to Primavera, Domingo Che. The group played the marimba. When the army came, they hid it in the jungle. They had a shelter in the jungle where they kept it. When the army withdrew, they took out the marimba, and played every Saturday. Every Saturday [or] Sunday, there was a dance. Everyone, children, women, old men, old women, everyone danced.

At times, it was sad, very sad, and at times, great happiness. When there were fiestas, the men went hunting and killed jaguars, killed wild pigs, *tepesquintle,* armadillo, and brought them to camp. We cleaned them and divided up the meat. A little for each one. Each prepared it [their own way], in *comales* or roasted. There were many animals. And the dances—there were always dances.

When there was no food, we looked for what we called *"quelite,"* a plant with big leaves. We gathered it, even if it was old. What we did was chop it up, put it with green bananas. We cut them in pieces and cooked them with the leaves. There was nothing else, not broth, nothing, only salt. We always had salt. We added salt, we added a bit of roasted corn with the bananas and leaves, boiled it, and gave a bit to each of the children. Just a spoonful, no more, because there wasn't enough. Everything we ate was measured. We prepared whatever we had. It was incredible how the people lived—so much suffering. Our clothes wouldn't dry; they stayed wet on our bodies. Now I suffer a lot. My bones ache; I have arthritis. There are days when it's bad, days when I'm very sick. That's how it is for me now. We think it's a consequence of living in the jungle in wet clothes, walking in the rain. It was hard.

Time went by. The multiparty commissions of Guatemala were organized. When they first came to visit the CPR in Ixcán, they saw how things were and began the steps to open up [dialogue with the outside]. I remember. My son, Alfredo, who now has a wife and child, was two months old. We were named to receive the commission. We all went. This was to come into the open.

We gathered firewood for three fires. They were told that where the smoke is, that is where the people would be. The smoke guided them. When we heard the helicopter, people wanted to flee for fear they would be bombarded. The children ran. They thought [the people in the helicopters] wanted to grab them. The mothers said, "They won't kill you. They've come to visit us, to learn [about us]."

The multiparty commission came to verify if it was true that there were civilians, because [the government] had said there were only guerrillas. When they came, they realized it was true.

I saw Bishop Julio Cabrera. Bishop Mario Molino cried bitterly to see the multitude of people. He said, "I didn't think there were civilians in this jungle. To see so many children." The children who ran, not to greet him, ran in fear that they would be killed. He said, "My heart is pained to see that there are civilians. We were told there were no children, just guerrillas. But today, I see . . . ."

Everyone organized [food]. There was cane, there was yucca, taro, bananas, fruit. They gathered everything. We made *tamalitos*, made jushte, everything. The bishops saw the food that we ate and tried it. They cried and said, "How did you live [here], with this food?" [One bishop] cried a lot and said, "It breaks my heart to see. I never imagined that people could live in the jungle with this food."

There were moments, as I said, sad moments, happy moments, difficulties, but we withstood it for fourteen years, living in the jungle. During fourteen years of struggle, we stayed. We had gone to Mexico, but we couldn't live in Mexico. We went to the hill in Center Thirteen, close to the border, and visited the sisters from Mexico. The brothers came. A priest came to visit us, and take us out. But we didn't go.

My husband had said to my uncle Angel, "I don't know why we live in the jungle, why we resist. Is it from stupidity? [Are we] fools? Why?"

My uncle answered, "No my son, you don't stay out of foolishness. You stay because you were chosen by God. Not everyone had the valor to resist in the jungle. You stay because you want to stay. You were free to go to Mexico. Why didn't you go? Because you didn't want to go," he said.

And so we were satisfied. We thought it was from God that we should stay, to resist, to put up with it. There were other things. I can't remember [it all]. Little by little, it comes back. We suffered, we lived through a lot. I remember coming here with our parents. We came for the good land. We lament that we couldn't be happy because of the war. That is a [very strong] memory, very sad. We hope it doesn't happen again.

Thanks be to God, my husband has had a lot of patience. Now he has enough money; there is enough food. We are at peace.

José Díaz Perez
Mayalán, November 2010 and November 2011

In Jacaltenango, my parents had very little land. They planted milpa on land the village owned. It was communal. My father got up early to watch his corn so the cows of the other villagers wouldn't eat it. He moved to Santa Ana Huista. Then it was all wilderness, from our village of Buena Vista all the way to the Mexican border. It was like here in the Ixcán.

My father and I worked on the road from La Democracia to Santa Ana. The labor was *mano de obra*—which meant that everyone had to work for the government two days a week, for the whole year, without pay. We built the road through the mountains with just shovels and pickaxes. Those who had money used the road, but us, never. Then the wealthy fenced in the land. They grabbed huge amounts, tremendous amounts of land. The large landholders dominated us in those times. The old campesinos suffered a lot.

I was eighteen then, and living with Luciana. We decided to come to Ixcán. We traveled to Huehuetenango and Barillas, where we rested for two days. Then, it was three more days to the First Center. The late Victoriano Matias was in charge there. We gave him our names and information. He said we had to find a padrino, a sponsor. The sponsor had to be responsible for us, and give us land where we could work until we got our own farm.

At that time, there was nothing here in Mayalan. The only ones here were the Monzóns. They gave us shelter. It was the year that a hurricane destroyed all the houses. You [the author] took us to the house where you lived. David gave us dry clothes, and Luciana (José's wife) put on one of Mirna's dresses. We stayed there all night. The roofs of the houses had blown into the arroyo. David was very good to us. He never left us. He didn't abandon us. He loved us very much.

The rivers were full of fish, but there was no salt. It was hard to buy anything. To get salt, sugar, or soap, we had to walk two or three days to Barillas. We had no money at the time, so I cut palm and carried it on my back. I sold it in Barillas and then bought the things we needed. We returned carrying sugar, salt, and lime. [Lime was used in preparing corn for tortillas.]

To make some cash, I went with Chus Camposeco to work on a finca south of here. We had to leave the poor women here. At times, there was no corn. But we managed. We built the airstrip. This was the first strip built after the one in the First Center. Later, we built the ones in Pueblo Nuevo, Cuarto Pueblo,, and Los Angeles. We were pressed for necessities, but we kept working on those airstrips, chopping down trees, digging out the stumps. The people were united then; the five co-ops were united. "For one day . . . for our children," I said to my wife. Even though there was no child yet, one has to have hope, just as our fathers had for us.

That makes me wonder now how it will be for our children. Will it be good or bad in these times? Not only for our children but for our grandchildren and great-grandchildren. When I was a child, one cent was a lot of money. There was the *tostón*, half a cent. I earned two cents a day, and my father eight cents. We worked from six o'clock in the morning to six o'clock in the evening. Now, even a child has five quetzales, or even twenty quetzales. We didn't know about money. No one knew how to read. We didn't know how to write. The only ones who could write were those who had children in school. Their children wrote for them. The majority of the people in the pueblo didn't know how to read. Everyone was blind, every-

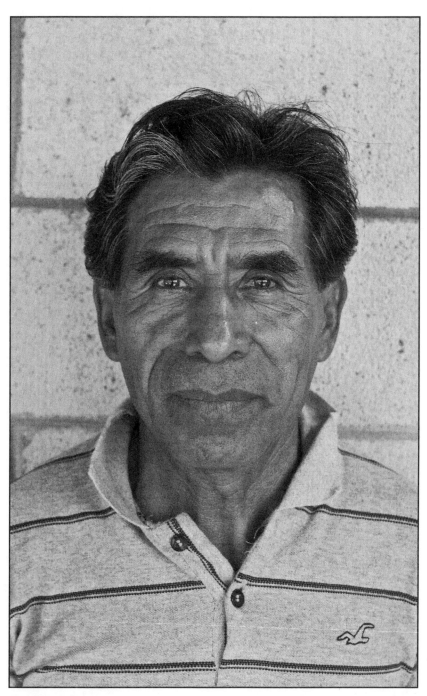

José Díaz Perez

one . . . blind. It was a way of domination, what they did before. In Mayalan, when I got my parcela in Mayalan, I signed with my thumbprint.

Working here in Ixcán, we were paid fifty cents a day. Padre Guillermo told us that there was an oil company where we could work and make some money. But there was no road from here to there. It was solid jungle. So padre made a "road" in the sky. We went in the airplane. When we worked at the oil field, we made one quetzal a day. One quetzal! But at the end of the month when it was time to pay, people who didn't know how to read received half their pay. Chus said, "Let's organize ourselves." There were just four of us. Most of the older people, about five hundred persons, didn't know how to speak Spanish. So we organized the first strike. They paid us, but then they got rid of us because of the strike. They wouldn't give us any work. I remember all that we suffered. There was nothing for our poor wives.

It was hard to be in Ixcán. But really, for me, this was the only way I could do it. It was the only way we could live. If we didn't do it, we would be working on the fincas again.

Then there was the war. We abandoned our houses but not because we wanted to. I left Luciana in Comitán, Mexico. Then I went back to Ixcán. I didn't see her for two years. I was here the whole time. I felt tremendous sadness because I'd abandoned my children and her. I'd abandoned them. But I understood, and she understood.

But this struggle opened my eyes, changed my way of thinking. I began to learn to read and to write. That gave me confidence. I learned here in the guerrillas. As I said, one learns from every experience, whether one wants to or not.

When my son was killed, I was here, "inside." They were resting on a path, and he forgot a grenade. He went back to get it so that he wouldn't be disciplined. He returned by another path. A booby trap exploded, and he was killed. He was buried there between Veracruz and Pueblo Nuevo. Who knows exactly where? They say it was in an arroyo, but which one? There are two arroyos there. It would be hard to find out. One would have to find the people who know.

After the war, someone came here to the house to tell us that there would be compensation for the victims of the conflict. We were thinking of going [to the meeting], but my other son, Oliver, said, "No. My brother doesn't have a price. He is not a beast that they can give money for him." The value of what he told me . . . that one is worth something . . . that gave me hope. We didn't have much communication with my son before he died, so this helped me a great deal.

I feel very hurt in the sense that I worked in the organization for so many years. They said, for example, that they would give us a house. To this date, it has not happened. I struggled without getting anything. Those who are *"de la pluma"* [literally, "of the pen," those who are literate] are getting something. But as I can't write well . . . nothing, nothing. Absolutely nothing.

But here (in Mayalan), there is still the co-operative. That is the root that Padre Guillermo left us. It is his seed that still exists. What he planted we won't lose. They now say we have many weaknesses because so many went back to their old towns. Now, others are entering—who knows if they are good or bad. Now, they are cutting down all the trees, but the root won't die. He is with us. He left us this land. We are doing fine. For many people, Padre Guillermo is not important, but for us, the elders, he is close to us. Why do we feel this so strongly? Because of Padre Guillermo, we are still alive. Because of him, we have land.

If it wasn't for him, I would still be going around in circles in my pueblo. Maybe I would be suffering in the fincas. For this reason, one laments his death. As he said, "I will die here." We also will die where he died.

Luciana Rojas Diaz
Mayalan, February 19, 2011

At times I dreamed of those who were fleeing, or of when I was in my own house. I didn't dream that the fleeing was from the army but just that I was running. I dreamed of extremely difficult places . . . in the jungle. I was running, but I didn't know from whom. It must have been the army. They made us run. When I awoke, I realized that I wasn't in my own house, and wondered when we would be able to return.

When the repression began, I never imagined that we would go to Mexico. Never, never did I think that. When things were very difficult, we went to the place where we were born. But what could we do? It was worse there than here [in Ixcán]. There, because of the kidnapping, the people had gone. They left before the civil patrols were formed. So when we got there, everything was desolate, the houses abandoned. At the end of 1981, the strong repression began. That is when we had to go to Mexico. We passed through the jungle and crossed the border. When we left, we didn't think much more would happen. I don't know exactly where we walked . . . here, through the jungle.

We were at the border for several days. The Mexican army was patrolling the river. They discovered that we were there. They took us, so they said, to Comitan. Since I didn't know that place, I never knew exactly where they took us. Then they left us at the Guatemalan border, at La Mesilla. So we went back again to our aldea.

In September of 1982, we went again to Mexico. The repression had gotten worse. The civil patrols began to be formed. They were looking for people everywhere, in the hills, in caves, in the riverbeds. So we had to go to Mexico. This time, we went through Nenton. We had to wait at the border, then we went through.

This was at the place where the smugglers from Jacaltenango always crossed. I wasn't with the refugees. I was with those who were "dispersed." It was difficult for me because, in the first place, I was without papers, as we say, *mojado* [literally "wet," implying someone who is in the country illegally], always very difficult because [it was] as if one was stealing, as if someone was doing something [wrong]. One couldn't move freely, or talk freely with the people for fear that they would "discover" you. So I lived closed in. If I went out to work, I had to be careful. The people that I came to know well told me to come, come to clean the house, to wash . . . . So I went. I had friends because people liked me, but I never had all the confidence that one has when one is free, when one is legal.

I spent some time in Comitan, outside the city. Later with friends, we went to San Cristobal. I was there several years, living on the edge of town. Then I was for two years in a small town in Oaxaca. I spent my years living among strangers. I got to know them a bit. They were sad when I moved to another place.

I took care of a house where there were things. It was very dangerous. I was risking my life, because the house was where we had things stored. When I needed to, I did errands outside the city, in the communities. The people that knew me, the neighbors, were friendly because I behaved well. But I couldn't put much trust in them. They were from Guatemala, from the small settlements near the border. I was never totally happy, always thinking of a return, to the point that I dreamed . . . . I passed fourteen years like that, my life going in circles.

Well, the violence has passed . . . . I think it won't happen again. When the first return happened, I was taken with a desire to come back. Mario was growing. I worried how this child would turn out if no one taught him to work. Oliver was unhappy that we weren't always at his side. He had gone to stay with some of my family in Chiapas. Mario was growing up without us being able to see him. While Mario was little, he was with me, but later, what would he do?

Luciana Rojas Diaz

We went to a refugee camp where my parents lived, to ask for shelter. We weren't sure what to do to enroll in another return. Go to COMAR [the Mexican Commission for Refugees], or to immigration, or talk to those who were organizing the returns. A family member accompanied me to the offices of ACNUR [the U.N. High Commission for Refugees] to tell them that I wanted to return to Guatemala. I explained to them that we weren't in a camp, that we moved around, we were dispersed, but that we wanted to return. They took note of us. Jose, my husband, came to the camp. We gathered there, me, him, Oliver and Mario, and awaited the day of return.

We came together with a large group but not until about the fourth or fifth return. Truthfully, we came with nothing, as we couldn't work freely in Mexico. Just the little bit we had gathered together. We were without papers. Mario wanted to continue studying, but he couldn't.

I was very content when I came here. I felt I was in my home. With difficulties but . . . . It was very difficult because one remembers how joyful it was when we first came. In the time of the conflict, we dispersed to different places, and returning is not the same. That is still painful. For example, I will never forget my son. The first of my sons died in the war. He died in 1987. Oliver returned but then left again. My daughter is alive, but it's not the same because we can't often see her. [She lives in Nicaragua.] Each one went where they could. They are grown. Each looks for their own way in life.

In that problem that happened [the war], one can't say that everything was lost, or that everything is all right. For example, people had this timidity, fear, so they didn't speak out. One needed to demand justice for the country. But one was afraid because of the repression. In broad daylight, one couldn't say anything. Now there is repression, but it's more political, more subtle. But more or less, we can say that one can speak out with more freedom than before. I think one can speak out more.

I am happy to be back. I never think of leaving. I feel that . . . I have confidence in being here. Here we will live with what God gives us in life.

Mariano Martín Pablo
Mayalan, June 9, 2010

My name is Mariano Martín Pablo, from Todos Santos.

One time, I talked with Padre Guillermo Woods, may he rest in peace. He had landed with the plane on the airstrip of Mayalan. When he came into the house, I was working in the co-operative store. He asked me what was wrong. I told him that I was sick with pain in my stomach. He said, "You are thin. Go see a doctor to examine your stomach and get cured."

I answered that I had been there. My brother's wife had just given birth. The midwives give a pill to ease the women's pain. So I went to get one, and I took it. But the pain in my stomach remained. I thought I would die. The midwives told me that it was not a natural sickness, that the problem was supernatural.

I told Padre that I was having many dreams about bad things, and was talking to people who were dead. I was talking on the radio in my dream. Father told me I had been dwelling on this too much, that it could harm my body because I was thinking about it so much. Or that there could be a worm or something inside my stomach.

"Are you married?" asked Padre.

"Yes, Padre. I am married in the church."

"Are you praying? Are you praying daily? I told him that at nightfall, I pray. I remember God, the heavenly father, but then the stomach pains come, and I have to lie down. Then I begin to pray again.

Father said, "Look, this is what is happening." You give a place for the pain in your stomach. For example, you're talking together with me in the house and someone else comes and interrupts, but you don't want to talk with them. [At night], you are praying, and the pain comes, like an enemy, and you stop talking to God. That is what's happening. Be calm, even in pain, but stop talking to the friend who interrupts. Don't make a place for the pain in your stomach. Be tranquil.

So I said, "Thank you very much, Padre. Thanks for your advice." And I said that I would obey.

When we finished, Padre said, "Look, Mariano, I'm going to Guatemala City." I entered the radio room and saw the crucifix hanging on the wall. I went out to the runway to talk to Padre. He was in the cabin of the plane. I waved my hand so he wouldn't start the engine. "What do you want?" he asked.

"Padre. Pardon me. I came to talk to you. There is a crucifix in the radio room. Can you lend it or sell it to me?" I asked.

"What do you want it for?" he asked.

"Padre, so I can see the image of the Lord Jesus Christ, and with what you said to me, ease my problem.

He answered me, "Mariano, when you see the image of Jesus Christ, will you believe? You are like Saint Thomas. You don't believe."

I was left without an answer. Then again, I said to Padre Guillermo, "Padre, better just sell me the crucifix."

"Ah, so you have enough money to buy God?" said Padre. I was left without an answer. So Padre said, "Look Mariano, if it is like that, go to the room, show me the crucifix from the window. Show me. I will nod my head." I went from the airstrip to the office. I took off the crucifix. It was nailed with a big nail. I grabbed the nail. It broke when I pulled it out. I took the crucifix to where he was on the runway in the plane.

"Padre, this is it," I said.

"Ah yes, that one. I hadn't remembered where it was. But look, that crucifix I received when I was ordained. They gave it to me when I

Mariano Martín Pablo

was assigned the mission that I now have. If it's like that, take it. Take it, and if you die before I do, the crucifix has to be returned," he said.

"Okay Padre, but if not?"

"Venerate it. Take care of it, and [respect] it," he said, "Take it." Our talk ended. I returned to the office. I was content with the talk I'd had with Padre Guillermo. I was happy he'd told me that I could have the crucifix. I was satisfied with the advice Padre Guillermo gave me. I am happy today that I carry the crucifix of the Padre. "Take care of it, and respect it."

I was in the house fifteen days after I'd spoken to the Padre about the situation with my health when I heard that his plane had crashed. It all happened like that. We had just talked, and then Padre died. I remember him very much and all the advice he gave me.

During the violence here in Guatemala, I carried the crucifix in my pack for three years here in the jungle of Ixcán. I never left it in the care of another, or hid or buried it. Finally, because of all the violence, I went to Chiapas, Mexico, for fourteen more years.

There were some letters here on the top of the crucifix. From carrying it on the run so much in the jungle, with so much noise, so much trouble, the image and the letters came unglued.

One day, I went to Guatemala [City]. I brought it with me. I went to talk with David [Hollstegge], and brought it so he could glue the image back onto the cross. He glued it, but the letters that were on top didn't stick. I don't know where they are. They fell off somewhere.

There was so much moving around in Ixcán and on the road. A lot of worries too. But the crucifix I carried at my side. I tied a piece of twine on the hands and at the belt, so it wouldn't be lost. Later, I glued it, and it is fine now. It doesn't fall off. Just the letters, I don't know where they ended up. But I knew the letters were an "I" and an "R." "INRI" it said. That is the story of the crucifix.

At this moment, may Padre rest in peace.

Natividad Jiménez Gómez
Mayalan, June 10, 2010

I come from Ixtuacán, Huehuetenango.

From their place of origin, my mother and father had gone to the coast where they were poorly paid. They were tired of the cotton fields, the coffee plantations. They were there when they heard about a place where they could live. And so all the family came to Ixcán.

We arrived with my papa in the year 1973. I was five years old. It was hard. It took two days to get from Barillas to Mayalan, crossing the Rio Ixcán on stones. Two days on foot, over the rocks and mud, carrying the cargo. Now it only takes two hours on truck or plane.

We came down looking for land, and we found some where we could live. We planted milpa, fruit, coffee, cardamom. My father and mother were happy to find land, to build a house to live in.

We suffered a lot. We hadn't brought anything. Although we didn't have money with which to buy chickens or pigs, we had enough to survive. When we arrived here, we began to plant corn. That was the first thing we planted in Ixcán. Corn, beans, rice, bananas, fruit, everything we needed to eat.

The cardamom and coffee began [to produce]. At that time, coffee and cardamom sold for a good price. We could sustain ourselves even better than before. We were happy, tranquil. We never thought we would have to leave this land again. Everyone happy, the people constructing houses. They were without worries.

I have many memories of Mayalan. When they began to divide the parcelas, it was very beautiful. They didn't give parcelas to persons who'd had some "problem." They only gave them to people who truly were in need. That is a powerful memory. I remember they had to first see if the persons got along, if they worked hard, if they really wanted land. If so, they were given land. But the people who were not serious, they weren't given land.

I wasn't in school when I was young. *Qué lástima.* How sad. The story is a bit hard. In truth, there was a school and all that, but . . . it's a painful story because they didn't put me in school. We didn't have brothers, sons, just us women. My father said, "Girls, why should they study? They are going to get married. Women need to learn how to work in the kitchen, not study." And so because of that, I wasn't in school.

Now that I am free of the influence of my father and mother, there are many opportunities. There was a program called CONALFA to educate women. After the return, now that I was a grown woman, I enrolled there. I have been able to get my sixth-grade diploma. I can write. I can't add so well, but yes, I can do it. Now, I can read and write—but not until now. Now, no one can tell me that I can't study. Now that I'm a woman, I want to study. Three years ago, I finished sixth grade. I'm learning, but the problem now is that I don't have a way to continue. So I stopped after sixth grade. Maybe I could continue *básico* [middle school]. It might be difficult, but I could continue studying.

After we had been living [in Mayalan] for six or seven years, the army began to kidnap the catechists and the directors of the co-operative. They made threats. They began to say, "They are guerrillas; there are guerrillas." A big problem began. They began to kidnap people, to "disappear" people. The army tortured them. They threw them from airplanes. They left them tossed in the pathways. They killed them. When the army arrived at the houses to take the people away, they said, "Those people support the guerrillas." They said a bunch of lies just to take advantage.

They would go to the parcelas looking for people and kidnap them. No one knew where the people went, where they ended up.

Natividad Jiménez Gómez

Even now, we don't know where many of them were taken, if they were abandoned, or buried, or burned. Many were never found . . . .

After that, the army changed its plan. Now, not only the men— they began massacring everyone, men and women and children . . . animals, everything. They even burned the houses. They didn't just [kill] but left the land completely barren, without animals or people. Those of us still alive had to go into the jungle. Some went into exile, others to their town of origin. Each one looked for a way to survive. That was our story.

My family, because of so much suffering from being under the control of one patrón, so much suffering from not having land to plant, so much from not having a place to put a house . . . . My father never thought of going to exile or going back to our *pueblo*. What my father said was, "We will be here in Mayalan. One day, we will get this land back again. If we go to Mexico, there will be no land. Who will give us land? If we go to our place of origin, it will be the same. It's better we stay. If the army kills us . . . . God will be with us if we live or die. Here we have to remain until we get back our land again."

Those were the thoughts of my father. And so, here we are again in Mayalan. We didn't go into exile. We were part of the CPR. We had to move and move, repeatedly, until the people returned to Ixcán. We arrived with them because my father wanted it like that.

It is the land, not anything else. It's not money. He had to defend his life here. He came to Ixcán for the land, and for the land, he would die. We also felt the same way. We said, "We can't leave as long as our father is here." So we stayed.

We were in the jungle for fourteen years, defending our lives. It was very hard. I've seen many things since I was a girl . . . . All the things that happened to me, times of sadness, times of happiness, times of suffering. In our house, there was a lot of happiness. We had many animals, chickens and pigs. At that time, there was no diseases. But now there are. I am a little sad because my chickens die from diseases.

We were a long time in the house, about seven years, living there peacefully. When the war came, we went into the jungle. In the jungle, I learned various things. There was no school. There was nothing. There were no pencils, there were no books, and so many children learned with just charcoal, with stones. There are stones in the river that we call *ashcal*. With them we began writing. We wrote on the stones with charcoal, and so I began to learn a bit, like how to write. Many began to learn to write. I didn't have much schooling but how I loved to join in. I learned many things there. And many who are now "professionals" learned there in the CPR.

People asked, "Why don't you learn to give injections?" "Maybe I will learn," I said. So I began. I couldn't write, I couldn't do anything, but I learned. I couldn't speak Spanish either, just [my indigenous language]. They taught me how to give injections. They taught me how to sew up wounds. They showed me how to give intravenous serum. I learned how to pull a tooth. I just watched what they did with the syringe, watched how much had to be given. I worked a long time in the CPR, more that five years, as a health aide. I attended to the people. When the planes dropped bombs, when children were injured, I gave first aid. I liked that very much.

I still appreciate it, because even now, it helps me a lot. I am teaching my daughters. "You have to do this . . . ." But my daughters aren't very interested. In the family, I'm the only one with much interest. I haven't done that work here because I don't have a diploma. But now I am thinking that I will study for my diploma and go to work.

Now I see that when the people returned again to Mayalan, it was a bit different. The parcelas of those who didn't come back were given to their children but not the children who truly wanted the land or wanted to work. There were children who no sooner got the parcela than they sold it again. That affected me. I don't approve of their doing that. They got the land through the suffering of . . . . Their fathers came down to Ixcán to free themselves from the power of a patrón. Now their sons are selling the land. It becomes a business. I feel very bad that they sell it, land that was gained by so much sacrifice.

Rodrigo Montejo Garcia
Mayalan, June 10, 2010

It was 1971. I came from Santa Ana Huísta, Huehuetenango. It was difficult because of the poverty. I remember Chus Camposeco from that time. He had been a catechist. He's the one who spoke about this place with Padre Guillermo.

The move down was very difficult. First, we spoke to various friends. Then we decided. We didn't have sufficient money for the trip here. That was one thing. The family did not want to move, even though we were so poor there. But we continued on. In Huehuetenango, we ran out of money. There was no more. I remember I had eight quetzales at the time.

We arrived in Barillas very demoralized. How could we get from there to [Ixcán]. We asked how far it was from Barillas. "Ah, it's a long way," they said. "It will take at least two days." We took our things down from the bus. That was another problem. We had brought so many little things. We had the grinding stone, the clothes, my son, and my wife. We didn't have a mule. There was no road for a car, so we had to carry what we could.

We left Barillas for Ixcán. In one day, we barely made half the distance. Eventually, we got to San Ramón. We arrived on the second day. I remember it was two in the afternoon on the eighth of June.

There was a small fiesta in Centro Uno. It is an important place in the history of this area. It was the fiesta of San Antonio. We arrived totally exhausted.

We suffered, we were sad, wondering what to do. They asked for a fee of five quetzales. We didn't have it. We had to earn it. I give thanks that there were many good people in the First Center. There was Vicente Carillo, who gave us some work. We didn't have one cent, not one, nothing. When we finished, we'd been paid twenty-five manos of corn, (one mano equaling five ears). Before, we'd earned five manos a day. We kept some of the corn to eat and sold the rest for our fee. That was the story of our trip.

Eight days after we arrived there, they named a sponsor who would find a place where we would live. They said, "Those who are going to receive you are in the Fourth Center. We all made it there. They gave us shelter. Each one of us went to a different place. There were cows and everything.

We worked on the runway in the First Center. It had been built, but what we did was fill in the low spots, improve it so the planes could land. After that, the Padre asked for someone to explore, to look for a location to make a town, Mayalan. They said it would be a big community, well populated.

We formed a group with Carmelino Recinos, a surveyor, to do a reconnaissance and see if it was a good place, if it had water, streams. We came here, where the runway is now. I remember Carmelino, who is on the other side, in Mexico, because of the violence. He measured the length of the runway. He made a map. We returned and gave the information to Padre Guillermo, telling him that the place was fine, that there was water, that it was a good place. There was a location for a runway, and for a town center. Afterward, we surveyed the town lots. Some months passed. Then Guillermo and David gave out the numbers of the lots, center by center. The Mames were in one center, the Kanjobales in another, a group of Jacaltecos were here. It was done like that. The decision took into consideration the different ethnicities.

Padre Guillermo said, "Here is where the runway will be." We built the runway. Working together, we cleared what is now the town center. We all came to dig out the stumps. We dug them out with picks, with axes, with whatever [we could find]. Some digging them

Rodrigo Montejo Garcia

out, others rolling them aside, others filling the holes with hoes. That is how we built the runway. It was the first runway I'd built. When that was finished, we began to organize for the arrival of [the others].

I remember when we went to do the community work in Pueblo Nuevo. It was a decision of the co-operative that when a runway was finished in one place, one had to be built in another. [When we finished] the runway in Pueblo Nuevo, we went to Cuarto Pueblo; after Cuarto, to Los Angeles.

In Pueblo Nuevo, I almost died. We were cutting trees down with axes. A big tree fell on me. It was an enormous tree, like a *ceiba*. I thought the trunk had hit me because I felt a heavy blow on my back. But no, the trunk fell to one side into the earth. Because of that, I am alive. Now it is different. There is technology, chain saws for example. It's easier. Before, we used axes to fell trees. Our situation was more difficult.

Padre brought good people to help. There was one of you gringos who was in solidarity. He went with us but barefoot. Barefoot! We all had boots; only he didn't have them. We said, "Look how he goes; and worse, he came from far away!"

Chus Camposeco said, "He wants to be one of us."

The others said, "Yes, look at him, barefoot." Chus, joking, told the others to take off their boots. We had enough *tamalitas* to stay for a week. There were no people there. We had to bring the tamales to eat. What work! He was one with us. In truth, it made us happy. These are the stories that we never stop telling. [The "barefoot gringo" would have been Bob Coe, a carpenter from Houston who was building the first co-op store/clinic in Mayalan.]

The runways were built not only by one community but by a union of all the co-operatives here in Ixcán. The airplane runways were very important because they were the means to transport the merchandise, to bring things in, and to sell our crops. So that is what Padre Guillermo gave highest priority. We made four runways. That's our story, some memories!

A few things about Padre Guillermo. I have many beautiful memories. He was always joking. After saying mass, he'd play with all the people, with everyone. He was always teasing. I don't know if you re-member. At times, when we had meetings, he sat on the bench to listen. No other priest would have spoken so openly. I'm a Catholic, but I've seen that priests are not all the same. I know this very well. I was young, twenty-five years old at that time. I remember all Padre Guillermo did. He played with a lasso, those thick lassos, and formed two groups [for a tug of war]. Groups of ten, fifteen, or twenty, depending how many there were. If one group won, there was no prize, just applause for the group. One time I remember the rope broke. Every one tumbled. There was a commotion. Both sides were all piled up.

One time when mass was ended, Padre came out and said, "Everyone come. Everyone come." Everyone gathered. He asked, "Who wants to wrestle with me? Someone as big as I am." And he rolled up his sleeves.

"Truly?" they said. "But who?"

"Come on. Whoever wants to wrestle me, come." And so there was Juan Cruz, and José . . . . I don't remember, someone from the B-8 [a surveyor's name for the location of one of the centers]. Those two were the biggest. They were from Todos Santos.

"Go on, José. José."

"No, Juan Cruz," they said. "He is bigger."

Juan said. "I'm willing." Padre took off his shirt; Juan did too. "Let's go." Padre grabbed Juan around the chest. Juan began to get mad. One grabbed the other by the belt. They struggled. It was a brawl. Juan Cruz was thrown down. Padre threw him. They rolled over and over. Padre was down. Three times, neither won. "*Bueno bueno, ya, ya, ya.* No more." A big applause. Those are the stories of the late Padre Guillermo.

I was just beginning to learn to be a catechist. He was always teasing the new catechists. He said, "I want seven catechists to come with me. Who will come?" The late Pascual Paiz, from Xalbal, was there. "I'll go," he said. "Me, me"

"Okay, get in [the plane]. We'll just go for a ride." But he wanted to tease them. They weren't accustomed to the airplane. He began to fly the plane in circles. The people were yelling. He came down steeply, went straight back up, "Padre, Padre, I am getting sick." Pascual was always doing something, misbehaving. He yelled, "Don't screw around, you crazy priest." And Father was laughing. When they came down, they couldn't walk.

When we went into exile, it was very different . . . . I had problems because during the violence—let's say the truth—the army persecuted us very much. Centro Estrellita was pretty much destroyed by the army because there were leaders there. Chus Camposeco was a leader of the co-operative. At that time, you couldn't find anyone who spoke more sincerely and openly about a co-operative, more socialist-minded, more communal. There was Chus and Manuel Ross, who was the overall president of the five co-operatives. And so the army concentrated their attention there. Which is to say, on Centro Estrellita and on ourselves. Someone said, "Go, go. You won't survive. The army is looking for you." A hundred soldiers came to my house. I left because of fear. What is there to say?

We fled. We were refugees a long time. We left as a family. I, my wife, and my brothers also, all of us. My mother was very old at the time; she was ninety-five years old. I remember the jungle. There were no pathways. We knew the army was patrolling the area. We walked for a long time. We went directly to Mexico. There were many people in the group who stayed in the jungle, who didn't want to leave. But we went directly to the other side of the border. It is only a few hours to the border. In the jungle, it was difficult. One of my sons cut his knee. He was ten. He was playing with a machete. We had to carry him, so it was difficult. We didn't arrive until the next day. But we didn't experience much of the difficult situation of those who stayed behind.

There are also good people in Mexico. They gave us work. We were there for a while.

Sebastian Sales Morales
Mayalan, June 11, 2010

We were in crisis and under a lot of pressure by not having land in the highlands. Even worse was the work we did on the coast, just working for the patrón of a finca. We began to understand that this struggle to get a piece of land was important. The Catholic Church commenced to do something for those who had no land, so this made us think about coming to Ixcán.

Sebastian Sales Morales

A Maryknoll priest, Padre Eduardo Doheny, led the poor, those people who needed these parcels of land. It was Padre Eduardo who founded the co-operatives. May he rest in peace.

In the beginning when the Ixcán was opened, we arrived at the First Center. There was no road from Barillas to Ixcán. We had to carry our cargo. Then we worked to construct some shelters.

Then came several people from Ixtuacán, several from Todos Santos, others, Kanjobales. Many of their names don't come to me. The late Esteban, Ramón, also Victoriano Matías, and Nicolás Mendoza, the late Juan Sales Ortíz, and Sebastian Ortíz, Alfonso Ortíz. I settled in the Second Center. In the Fourth Center were the late Esteban and Ramón Maris.

Centro Dos belonged to Mayalan. When it was first settled, Mayalan was called Center 20. Padre Eduardo named the settlements after places in the Bible, beginning with Centro Uno. He named the First Center, Belen [Bethlehem], and Center Two, Nazareth; Center Three, Cana; Center Four, Jerusalem. Like that, the names . . . . Center Thirteen was named Jordan. It was very significant, remembering where Christ had worked. It was similar, a new land, a promised land for the poor here in Ixcán.

Remembering Mayalan, there was much happiness; it was lively. There were so many animals. In Centro Uno, there were quantities of cattle on the banks of the river, and the Rio Ixcán had so many fish. A fish named "Los Coches," they passed by, swimming like they were airplanes. It was a happy life because the animals came close. And the birds, like the toucans, the *pavo reales,* the *paisanes.* It was a joy. The parakeets were close. It was virgin jungle, beautiful jungle. And the *guacamayas* . . . huge quantities of guacamayas, building their nests in the branches of the ceibas. They were great birds. But now we don't encounter them. They are disappearing. In reality, it was a beautiful life, and the milpa . . . . Just clear the jungle and work on the bottomlands . . . so much nightshade, squash, beans . . . . It was a good life. The seed only needed watering at the beginning when it was planted. It grew, it gave forth. Now it is different; you have to fertilize and watch it a lot. In those times, it was a good life.

The animals came close to us, especially jaguars. The jaguars visited us regularly. They didn't let us have dogs or chickens. They liked to take them. In those days, there were many in the jungle.

In 1967, Padre Eduardo had an accident. One of the fiestas that Padre Eduardo celebrated was the fiesta of Holy Trinity. On that day, we were celebrating the Holy Mass in the *galera* [a large open shed]. My wife and I were at the Mass. Mass was just beginning with the entrance songs, singing "Señor Ten Piedad," Lord have mercy.

There was a tall tree. No one had thought to take out this tree when they built the galera. Suddenly a strong wind came and the tree fell. God didn't want his sons to die, because if the tree had fallen directly on the church, it would have been a huge disaster. But as God is great, the tree fell a bit to one side. Only a branch hit part of the galera. Padre Eduardo had run in that direction with a brother who was from Chiantla. My wife and I separated. She went one way, I another, in fright . . . .

Later when the rain diminished, we looked around. Where were the people? The Padre, where is the Padre? He was trapped under a branch. It had knocked him out. We began to get it off of him, but something was stuck. We couldn't get the branch off. Everyone pushed and squeezed the Padre. The pulling hurt him. It was impossible to get the tree off him. We wanted to help him quickly. He had a bad wound on his head. Padre was unconscious. We took him over the bridge to his house. When we got there, we began to call on the communication radio to advise the Maryknolls at the apostolic center in Huehuetenango. They called Padre Guillermo to come and get him the next day with the airplane.

The people passed the night watching and praying for Padre Eduardo. The person from Chiantla, who was hurt badly too, died during the night.

Padre Woods, may he rest in peace. He had a lot of courage to land because the runway in the First Center was still not completely "normal." It had been recently repaired, but Padre Woods was able to land and take Eduardo out in the plane, and he survived.

Padre Guillermo took over in 1969. He put the people in charge of the work. He began to organize and assign the jobs. Miguel, I remember that Padre Guillermo was quick to get things done. He had contact with Alas de Esperanza, Wings of Hope, and he brought various pilots [to Ixcán]. There is one buried in Centro Uno. It is pilot Juan Stork. We still remember him, There were several. I don't remember all the names. Miguel, you were in the team. David was in charge of the surveying, and he got Madre Juana from Jacaltenango to work with the health aides.

To finish the story, the army began to spread rumors against Padre Woods, that he was a leader of the guerrillas, that he was forming small cells. They put him on a blacklist. But in the end, he continued working, doing so many things here. Flying out the sick, continue seeking the land titles in the name of the co-operative. He fought hard.

And so Padre met with his death. On the nineteenth of November, we had our last communication with him. I was on the radio in Huehuetenango when he called, "Okay, Sebastian, I'm going to Ixcán." If I'm not mistaken, it was two in the afternoon, or between two and two-thirty. He left Guatemala City for Ixcán. "I'm going to land in Xalbal and then go to Pueblo Nuevo," the padre said.

"Okay, Padre, then we will communicate at six." We communicated on the radio at six in the morning, twelve, and at 6 p.m. His last words were, "We'll talk in the evening."

That evening, I tried to make contact with him, and there was no reply. I asked Pueblo Nuevo, I asked Mayalan, I asked Xalbal, I asked Los Angeles, and no one had news of Padre. The radios shut down at eleven at night on the nineteenth. On the twentieth, at about four-thirty in the morning, I got up and went to the man in charge of civil aviation. I asked him for information about Padre Woods, but there was nothing. Then he told me, a bit quietly, like a secret, "Look, a notice came from Peten, informing us that TG-TEX [the call letters of his plane] has burned up in San Juan Coatzal."

My soul left me when I heard that. I said, "Thank you." I sent the notice to the co-operatives, and I went to the Maryknoll central house to ask them if they already knew.

"Yes, we received the news. We know . . . ." So we knew that Padre was dead, and that he was with other persons. I think there were three other people with Padre Guillermo. We couldn't be sure. Apparently, they were coming to help here in Mayalan with Proyecto Ixcán Grande, but they ended up dead.

The question arose about whether to move him to Huehuetenango. Others said it would be better if he went directly to the United States. But his mother said he wouldn't have wanted to go to the United States but to remain in Guatemala. And so he stayed in Huehuetenango for the time being, and later, it would be decided what should be done. That is how it was at the death of Padre Guillermo Woods.

We left our house on the twenty-fifth of May of the year 1982. Mayalan was destroyed by the hands of the army. They had burned all the houses, all the offices, everything. We were escaping; we had to run. Then helicopters began to arrive. They began to search at night. It was a clear night. There was a full moon. I remember because we couldn't light a fire in the jungle; the smoke would give us away. So we had to carry on. The helicopter was circling over Mayalan, looking for more guerrillas. There were so many people walking out at that time, more than five hundred. There was a crossing over the Rio Pescado south of Mayalan, close to where the road bridge is now. The hamáca was a little bit downstream. There was one hamáca on the path to Pueblo Nuevo and one on the way to Veracruz. The one we were looking for was the one that led to Pueblo Nuevo. We were trying to escape to the Mexican border.

The army, having finished with Mayalan, was hidden. As we were crossing, they clashed with the guerrillas at the ford across the Rio Pescado. We ran into the fight. It was fierce. We hid in the jungle.

My daughter, María Floridalma, who is here in the corridor weaving, was injured. There were explosions, bursts of gunfire. Her mother was carrying her in her arms. She was two years old. We didn't notice at the time, but when we arrived in Mexico, we saw that María and her brother had auditory problems.

The problem was caused by the noise. We didn't know that when something explodes close by . . . like happens with the fish when you throw a bomb in the water . . . . The fish are battered senseless, even though they weren't touched. The noise is what does the damage. And so that is what happened to her. Because she was a small child, she must have had her mouth closed tightly. She didn't know that the noise would rupture the eardrums. It was more from the noise than from the fright.

In Mexico, we found hearing devices for the children, but at times, there weren't any batteries. At times, the apparatus made noises, and so sometimes, they didn't use them.

Floridalma only completed fourth grade. Her brother completed middle school. They made an effort, but having this hearing impairment . . . . But she can talk and work. What she does now is make weavings for a living. If someone orders a *morrál,* she can make one in two or three days, and so she can support herself.

Now what most impairs us and is affecting many people is trauma. This is what harms us now. Because we were left on our own, the events remain in our lives, and the majority of us are suffering it.

I have strong feelings about Padre Woods. He was always smiling, always very active. He helped me escape from slavery. I was uneducated. I had done two grades in school. But, thanks be to God, he inspired me. He led me to learning. In 1969, he arrived and encouraged the catechists in their formation. He took us to the Apostolic Center in Huehuetenango, and at that time, he gave me permission to visit the sick carrying the body of Christ. He said to me, "You are the deacon of Ixcán." I still remember all that Padre Guillermo did. It was very important for us, even though there are some who put him down . . . not all. . . . The work, the preparation, his heart was for the good of all. I get emotional when I speak about Padre Guillermo, or Padre Eduardo.

I remember the work of the pilots, the work of David. It was a grand sacrifice, a grand thing that was done for Ixcán.

The refugees, those who returned, are denounced for the same reason as Padre Guillermo Woods was. They say that we were guerrillas.

They call us that, but our struggle is in accordance with the teachings of God. God does not agree with the injustice. We want justice. Who are they who deny us justice? Those in power always exploit us. Maryknoll began the project of Ixcán Grande with a parcela of four hundred cuerdas for each one. That is an example of justice.

Thanks be to God that we weren't forgotten after our return. The Catholic church was rebuilt here in Mayalan. It was rebuilt in San Lorenzo. It was rebuilt in Pueblo Nuevo, in the center of Candelario de los Martires, and in Cuarto Pueblo, and in Los Angeles. The Maryknolls did not forget to rebuild the work that Padre Woods began.

The children I have were born in Ixcán, and are now finding their way. They are not professionals but more or less . . . . Not one does not know how to read and write. That was a gift from Padre Guillermo Woods. From the beginning, he had the idea to push education—because with education, only with education, can we learn many things, the laws, the word of God, and things we meet on the road of life. That is the bread of knowing how to read and write.

María Floridalma Sales Ordóñez
Mayalan, February 19, 2011

When I was little, two years old, we left Ixcán. We were guided by some guerrillas. I grew up in Campeche. I realized that I couldn't hear much. I went to a doctor in the city of Campeche. They gave me a hearing aid. They asked my parents how this happened. My parents replied that I was two when we left Ixcán, and some soldiers dropped bombs right beside us.

We returned in 1995, and I was in school until the fourth grade. I didn't continue studying, and began to work with my parents in the parcela. I can't work elsewhere because of the problems with my hearing. In the house, I sew *morráles* in order to help pay for my son's education. I'm happy with his life.

I am now twenty-nine years old. My boy, Alejandro, is twelve.

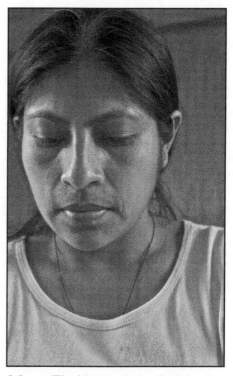

María Floridalma Sales Ordóñez

Valentin Juan Domingo
Zunil, June 11, 2010

In those days, my eight-year-old child was in the hospital. My daughter had been playing. A stick hit her leg and broke the bone. I took her to the hospital in Huehuetenengo. She was there for eight months.

When she got out, I communicated with Padre Guillermo Woods, and he brought her to Ixcán in the airplane. There were other sick people. As I was healthy, there wasn't room for me, only the sick ones. He brought them here to Mayalan. It was a Friday. I was returning on the road to Barillas when I heard that Guillermo Woods had died.

Because of that, I remember Guillermo Woods with sadness. We'll never forget all he did. He carried out the sick . . . and brought them back.

We were in Mexico less time than other refugees. We left Guatemala in 1982, and returned in '88.

My family went around just talking like Mexicans. They didn't remember how the culture was here in Guatemala. We talked to Monsignor Julio Cabrera, of Quiche, during his visit to Quintana Roo. My mother, my wife, and I thought it would be better to return. We made plans. I went to say goodbye to the bishop of Quintana Roo in Chetumal. He blessed me and sent me off. "If the war continues, the door is open for you." So I said goodbye and came here directly. It was just me and my family. I didn't join a group.

ACNUR gave us a van. They took us to Comitan. From Comitan, we came in a truck to Huehuetenango. We were there two days and

Valentin Juan Domingo

then went in another truck to Coban and Veracruz. From there, we walked to Mayalan and Zunil. We carried our things on our heads. There was no road, so we carried everything.

When we arrived in Zunil, there were six families living there. Later, we communicated with those of Cabrican and Huitan. We traveled to visit them, and went to the Diocese of Huehuetenango to see the bishop. I went to tell him that we had arrived again in Zunil. Through the church, we could communicate with more people, get news of the others who had stayed in Guatemala, and of those who were in Mexico waiting for the signing of a peace treaty.

And so we returned. But one of my daughters didn't like it here in Guatemala, and returned to Mexico. She married a man from Villahermosa, Tabasco. They live in Benamérito. Her papers are Mexican. Her children are Mexican. She is Mexican now.

In 1989, I was shot. The guerrillas? I don't know who shot me.

The army couldn't leave their fort. When they did, there would be a firefight. Since they couldn't go out, they sent us to see what was happening around the town. We were just civilians, unarmed. The soldiers left us free to go to our parcelas. "Just advise us if you see anything." But the guerrillas didn't want that, so they shot us. Since we were under the control of the army, they assumed we were against them, so they attacked us. There were just four of us. One was hit in the hand, and I in my leg. One bullet went through; the other stayed in my leg. I carried that bullet for a year.

The army sent me to the military hospital in the capital. I was only there four days, and then they discharged me. Those of ACNUR let me rest for another twelve days in the capital, in a hotel. Then the U.N sent me here to Mayalan in an airplane.

That was my suffering at that time.

Juan Silvestre Quiñones
Mayalan, November 20, 2011

We were living here in Mayalan when we bought a marimba in Barillas. We'd had it about a year when we sold it to Don Cristobal from Cuarto Centro. It didn't work well; the keys were out of tune. It didn't make good music. Now we were without a marimba. People were accustomed to hearing the music, so they began to ask us, "Jacaltecos, when are you going to get another marimba?" But we weren't thinking about it.

Later, we got together, my brother Chus Quinones and Pancho Ross. Also my friends Julián Ross, Manual Ross, and Julián Calmo; they have passed away. "What should we do, bros? Everyone is complaining because we don't have a marimba. When will we buy another?"

"But there is no money," we said. "What can we do?"

"Look, now is the time of *achiote*. Let's cut and shell them, then sell them here. We will get fifty quetzales each. We have the drums, and we can buy the violón. So we decided to buy the marimba.

We began to get excited. "Let's don't say anything; let's just go and buy it. When the others learn about it, the marimba will already be here. They'll just hear it." We went together to an aldea named Yalah, close to Jacaltenango where the marimba makers were. I went by myself to Jacaltenango, to a person named Baltazar.

I asked him, "Do you make violóns?"

"I am the one who is making them."

"And how much is a violón?"

"Where do you live? I haven't seen you here for a year."

"I am from Mayalan, from Ixcán."

"Brother, you went there! And your family?"

"I have them there with me."

"Ah, that's great. So, just for you, I'll give you the violón for eighty quetzales." In those days, it was still inexpensive.

"That's fine," I said.

The others were in charge of bringing the marimba from Yalah to Barillas. We agreed to pick up the marimba on the date of the third of May. I stayed in Barillas to wait for them. Those who went to get the marimba were Rodrigo, Julián, Manuel, Ricardo, Manuel Ross, Pancho, and Chus. We met up in Barillas.

I had a friend, Juan, in Barillas. He asked us, "And what are you here for, my friends?"

"We came to pick up a marimba. We ordered one from Yalah, and they're bringing the violón from Jacaltenango. We came to wait for them.

"Ah, okay. It is the fiesta of the third of May here in Barillas. I like how the Jacaltecos play. Can you do me the favor? Here there are *marimbistas*, but they're not the same as the Jacaltecos.

His wife said, "Ah, those from Jacaltenango! I love how they play. It's pure heaven, just hearing their music; it makes one want to cry."

Then Juan said, "I'm going to ask you to play. Although you are from another pueblo, and I'm from here, we are brothers. We are all sons of God. Can you play for a few hours? Don't worry about food; you can eat and sleep here. And will you do us the favor of playing for two hours in the church?"

"That's fine. No problem."

"Ah, good. The people from here will be surprised to hear the music. Can you play the song called 'Lisha'?" he asked, "and another called 'When Mali Cries,' and 'Ixtia Jacalteco'?"

We inspected the boxes and the keys, checking to see if there was any torn cloth. We played the first song on the porch of the man's house. He jumped up. "Yes, that's it. Ah, the music that the Jacal-

Juan Silvestre Quiñones

tecos play! The 'Ixcánecos,' " he said. "They're from Jacaltenango, but they are a band from Mayalan. They have a great band."

It was about eight at night. "Now let's go to the church." Someone was selling fireworks. Juan bought about ten dozen of them, and then we went to the church. The people were surprised. In Barrillas, they don't celebrate as we do in Jacaltenango. In Jacal, when there is a novena, two people carry the big marimba, and another carries the small one. We played as we walked along. When we got to the church, the people crowded around and wouldn't let us stop. "Play another, *muchá*. Play another! How did those Jacaltecos get here? Who brought them?"

Juan explained, "These are my friends. When they first went to Ixcán, I gave them shelter. They came to ask for a place to stay while they waited for the marimba. Tomorrow, they will go to Mayalan. They are making us a gift of the music." And so we played for almost three hours in the church. At about one in the morning, we stopped.

We got up at five and put on our head straps. There were no trucks, and there was still no road. And so we walked, each one with his cargo. Arriving at the Rio Ixcán, we asked, "How will we get across?" In a canoe? Will it hurt the marimbas? "No, we'll be careful." First, we took over everything else, then I and another crossed with the marimba. So that the marimba wouldn't fall out, I lay down in the canoe on my back with the marimba on top of me. I held onto it, and we crossed.

About three in the afternoon, we got back here. We took the marimba to the house of the late Julián Ross. We began to put it together; we had removed the keys to carry them. No one knew that the marimba had arrived.

Manuel Ross was one of the directors of the co-op here. He went to Guatemala [City], and there he bought two *tumbál*, round and high like this. The drum set we had. There were eight of us. We began to play in the evening. But let's not play a complete piece, just practice. When the sons of the late Alejandro Recinos heard the marimba, they began to crowd around. "*Mucha* [bro], why didn't you tell us you were going to get another marimba? This one sounds so good." When the tenth of May arrived, we played in the *bodega*. People began to take up a collection to pay for music. On Saturday evenings, we all came to practice. That's how we brought the music here.

When we came back on the "return," we brought another marimba, which we bought in Campeche. In Mexico, we'd played with other friends. We played there in Victoria. We were Don Basilio Paz from Victoria, Pedro Jacinto from San Lorenzo, his son, my late brother Chus Quiñones, Mauricio, Sebastian, Julián, my three sons, and myself. Some stayed there in Victoria, two went to San Lorenzo, and the rest of us came here—my late brother Chus and Mauricio, Sebastian, and Julian. "Mauro," my son, liked to play marimba very much. We played for about two years. Then my late brother Chus was taken. My two sons were taken. I was left alone with Mauro. And so the music ended.

In Mexico, a snake bit me, one of those with four nostrils. They call it the *barba amarilla*. A big thick one, almost two meters long. I was walking in the fields with my sons. Sebastián was in front. I told him to get behind me. There was a narrow path in the bushes and a lot of branches lying on the ground. I thought it was a log. When I stepped on it, it moved, and the head appeared. It bit me through my boot. I had told my son Mauro the story of a friend in my village. The man was bitten. What he did, he cut himself. Mauro remembered this.

"We'll cut your leg here so the venom comes out," he said. So he held my leg and took a machete. It made a noise when it hit the bone. We each grabbed my leg. When we let go, poison came out with the blood.

In a moment, I was up on my feet. The swelling only got to my knee. Above that, there was nothing. I walked about two hundred meters, limping with a staff. After twenty minutes, I began bleeding from my gums. After twenty-five minutes, I began to vomit blood. This happened in 1983. It was the tenth of September when that animal bit me. They brought me to where I was staying with the Mexicans in Playón de la Gloria.

My friends took me to the clinic in Mijón. They only gave me an IV. There was no medicine. It was about ten in the morning when the snake bit me, and about 2 p.m., I was vomiting blood. I passed all the night vomiting blood. At around nine or ten in the morning, the airplane arrived and took me to Comitan. At that time, they still flew into Margarita. When the plane was descending, they opened the window, and I vomited. They said, "This man is going to die." Landing in Comitan, the plane bounced three times. That's how I felt it. They got me down and put me in a car. At ten thirty, I arrived at the hospital in Comitan. I lost my mind. I thought I had died there.

All day, I was dead, all night. I woke up about five in the morning. My foot was hurting. I wanted to speak, but I couldn't talk. There wasn't enough blood. Three days after I arrived at the hospital, I was still in the bed. There was the nurse watching to see if I would awaken or not. I awoke. "¡Ay! My God." When the nurse saw that, she got up. . . . "Don Quiñones, Don Quiñones."

I could barely talk. She went out, running. In a moment, the doctors came in. They took out one IV, leaving another. They put medicine in the drip. My foot felt hot. I didn't feel anything in the other. Later, on the third day after arriving at the hospital, all the flesh fell off. Only the two bones were left. On the tenth of September, I was bitten; on the sixteenth, they cut off my leg. Then they sent me to a hospital in Puebla, Mexico. I was in the Puebla hospital for six months. I returned to the refugee camp. There I began to have pain. They cut my leg three times. Here, here, and here. Each time, they cut farther up the leg. First below the knee, then just above the knee, then mid-thigh. Three times. But I give thanks to God that I was saved.

Now my work is making pack saddles. I just sold some. I had eight made, but people bought them. There is only one left. It is tough work, but I give thanks to God that I am alive.

Ramón Mendoza Ramírez
Mayalan, February 20, 2011

[In 1990 I interviewed a young Ramón in a refugee camp in Mexico for a video I was making about the situation in the Ixcán.]

When I remember you, I think of that interview. At that time, I didn't know how to speak Spanish, only Mam. When you interviewed me, I couldn't say anything. Spanish was a little complicated for me. When I was six, seven, eight, I didn't speak it at all. I went to school without understanding the teacher. But I was learning a tiny bit. I learned to read and write. I learned Spanish when I was twelve years old.

Leaving the country gave us many experiences, and now we hope that with what we learned, we can construct a new reality for our children. We suffered much on the journey from Ixcán to Mexico and back, but now things are improving.

Our parents struggled hard. We remember the work Padre Guillermo did for us. Because of him, we have our lands. For that, he is always present and alive with us.

When we had returned from Mexico, some of us younger ones didn't want to be here. Some went back again to Mexico, because there were comforts that didn't exist here. There, there wasn't mud, Here, there was, and one had to walk a lot. One had to make a big effort to go and return from the parcela for work.

I was named an Education Promoter when I got back to Mayalan. Our organization of teachers is called Asociación de Educadores Nor-Ocidentales [Northwest Educators Association]. The Guatemalan government gave us training toward an equivalent to graduating with a teaching certificate. And so I graduated as a teacher. Then I went to the university and studied sociology, through the Universidad Polytécnica de Quito, in Prodessa, Guatemala. But at the moment of graduating, the university said it would cost forty-five hundred dollars for me to do the thesis. Since I'm the first son, I used my salary to support the family and to help my brothers in school. I didn't have it. But I had heard that it was good to go to the States, that there was work, and that one could get ahead. So I got it into my head to go to the United States illegally.

I didn't have problems traveling through Mexico because I had lived there. I didn't have problems at the border either. I walked two nights and a day. The desert was hot, very hot. You don't know if you will make it to your destination. People had said to me, If you are going to go, you have to think about it once, twice, three times. There are many people who make it and others that don't. There are many who go with a mountain of hopes on their back, but the desert cuts short the realization of dreams. So I went thinking of two things: If I go and remain in the desert, I die. But in Guatemala, there are no opportunities. So I had to go. On the way, I saw people who had recently died and people who had been dead a while, maybe fifteen days. That causes fear, but it gives you more courage, and you think, I have to do the utmost. Behind, there is a family who waits for something from me. That inspires you, and you continue on.

And it all worked out. I arrived in Tucson without problems. The people who were waiting picked us up. They locked us up for two nights until someone paid. A friend paid for me, and then we went directly to North Carolina. The *coyote* told us that we were lucky because no one had stopped us. There are many who have had bad luck crossing the desert, or when they go by car to their destination, the immigration catches them and sends them back.

The first days were spent working in the fields: squash, tomatoes, chile, everything that grows in the country. But they didn't pay very

Ramón Mendoza Ramírez

well. We worked from five in the morning until five at night, and didn't get nearly anything. So I thought, why do this? Because I didn't have money to pay for my studies. I looked for something else. From Carolina, I went to Florida. I still didn't have much luck. I was there six months and then went to Atlanta. In Atlanta, I worked doing landscaping with a Brazilian. Now I could send some money to my family. My family had suffered a lot because I had taken what money we had. They were left without anything. I made a bit in Atlanta, saving some; the rest I had to send to my family.

At that time, my father was also in Atlanta. You heard it said, in the United States, there are "the corners." The corners are where people go to wait for someone to come looking for workers. I was on a corner with my father. Someone came: "I need two people to work. Come with me."

"All right," I said, "but I want him to come with me. He's my father."

"Okay, both of you come." When we got in, he asked, "What do you know how to do?"

"We can do any kind of work. Lay bricks, carpentry, whatever."

"Okay." When we had been in the car one hour, he said, "I am a policeman."

"Police," said my father in our language, in Mam. "The police have caught us." He continued talking about the police. We thought we'd been caught. But no, after two hours, we arrived at his house. He introduced us to his father, his mother, and to his brother, who was a doctor.

He said, "This is my mother's house. This is where you are going to work." What a relief. It was a policeman, but he wasn't going to arrest us. He was a very good policeman, a good man also. At eleven, he gave us something to eat. There are many good people in the States. We worked planting flowers and laying a stone floor. They said to us, "As long as you are good, as long as you don't do anything illegal, you can be here."

Later, work became scarce. Sure, there was work with the companies, but you needed documents, and as we didn't have any, we had to depend on the luck of the corners. Once I was on the corner when an old man arrived, white, with white hair, everything white. He said, "Do you want to work for me?" I was afraid of the immigration, even though I had worked for a policeman.

"What work?"

"Do you want to work?"

"Yes."

"Okay, get in."

"But what work?"

"Get in. Later I'll tell you."

As I needed work, I said, "All right. I'll go."

"But it is not here; it's in Alabama."

I thought, "Now what will I do?" But since I needed the work . . . . "Lets go to Alabama." I got in the car. There, I encountered a tall, strong man. I thought, Now what have I done? Well, now I am here . . . .

He said, "Since you're going to Alabama, take your things." We went to the apartment. I didn't have much, a small pack with two or three pair of pants; that's all. He asked, "Do you have money?" I didn't have a cent.

"Okay." He went into a gas station, bought a few things, and gave some to me. When we arrived, he said, "This is going to be where you work. Some of the men have been here five years, others ten years." The one who has been here ten years makes a thousand dollars a week."

A thousand dollars a week, I thought—that's money.

"You are going to wash the dishes." I'd come to a restaurant to work. That day, as I washed plates, I calculated that we had attended about three thousand people. It was extremely hard.

No, this work isn't for me. It's so difficult, better if I go. But how could I go? I didn't have a car, and the men who were there didn't know me. My father had stayed in Atlanta.

My boss said, "I will pay you $280 a week." I thought: $280, it is very little. "I will see how you work. Next week, I'll pay you more. It depends on how you work." The first week, I thought this work is not for me. I'm leaving. I'll go back to Atlanta to see what happens. But I couldn't go to Atlanta. I wanted to take a Greyhound bus, but someone said, "If you go on Greyhound, and the immigration boards it, they will catch you, and you'll go back to your country." So I stayed there. After two weeks, three weeks, a month, the boss raised my salary $20. I made $300. I sent it to my family. After two months, he raised my pay $20 more. Now it was $320. I asked the others how much they made. One made $700, another $800. The cook made $1,000—the "first" cook. So I said to myself, I'm going to make it to cook also, and I stayed. They began to pay me $400, $500, $550. We worked well and did a good job. My work was steady. The little I sent to my family was acceptable; it was good. But we are now talking of the third and fourth year of my being in the United States.

Because I worked very hard, was very fast and efficient, other friends found me work. They called me from another restaurant in Florida, and said, "Are you Ramón? We have heard you are a good person and work hard. We want you to work for us." I was now the second cook; we called it *segundón*.

"And what position would I have there?"

"I want you to be *primerón*, first cook. I didn't think twice. I went alone. The first time I entered the restaurant, I came in the front door. The next day, it was the back door. And in all that time, I never entered through the front door, just the back. Things stabilized for me. I made a lot of American friends.

The restaurant where I worked in Florida, called La Hacienda, was good. I recommend it. Nothing happened there, nothing. All the men working there had a vehicle. The owner had the license numbers of our cars. He told the police that he had so many workers. So if there was a problem, the police would call the owner. He was well known; he was someone who helped the schools. He said to us, "You behave, no drinking, no problems—that way nothing will happen to you. Okay?" We always behaved. As it was a small town, nearly everyone knew us. There were other Mexican restaurants, but La Hacienda was well known, and so people always asked for us. Everything was good. I was motivated. I will stay one year more and in that year save a bit of money, finish my studies, and provide a good opportunity for my children to study. I will build a house there in Mayalan. Everything was good.

The day they got us was a Wednesday. That was the day I had to pay the bills for the telephone, garbage, the rent, and other things. I had a break at 1 p.m. I entered again at 3 p.m. The owner said the police were there. "You decide if you run or not." The man who was in the kitchen when I got there said, "Ramón, the immigration is here. Let's go."

I said, "No. I can't do that. If I go and it isn't the immigration, who will prepare the food?" People were waiting. It wasn't unusual to see the police around because they dined there. This day, the restaurant was full of police. They always came to eat there. I said, "No, it's nothing. They're just here to eat." But it was not just to eat.

The friend said, "You want to do what's right; me, I'm going." He opened the door. The police tried to grab him, but he escaped. The girl who seats the people, the hostess, ran out and got in his car. The police wanted them, but they didn't follow them.

I thought, Now we're caught. I was so angry when I realized it. The policeman who interrogated us was an Italian. He asked why we were here. We said, "We are here because in our countries, there doesn't exist the possibility of offering something to our children." I said, "I am here because I have a family, and where I live, there are no opportunities. And also, I want to finish my studies."

He said, "No. Why did you come illegally?"

And I said, "I ask the same of you. I think you came here illegally too." This made him mad.

He said something like, "Be quiet or everything you say will be held against you." This frightened me, but it also gave me courage. This guy, why does he act like that if he too wasn't born here. He's Italian. I didn't know if he was Italian, but his Spanish accent seemed to me to be Italian.

At about three in the afternoon, we were seated in the front. The clients were arriving. All the clients were mad at the police. The police interrogated about ten persons who worked in the restaurant. They took my driver's license and my Guatemalan I.D. They took my wallet.

I hadn't sent money to my family yet. I was going to send it the following week, so I had $800 in my wallet. It was my salary for two weeks. I had paid the bills and other things. This was the second time I used the front door. I entered for the first time by that door, and I left for the last time by that door. The first time, when I arrived, and the second time, when they deported me. It's a bit, I don't know . . . ironic?

They took me to the jail. I couldn't believe it. The restaurant owner said, "You have done nothing wrong. The only thing is that you are here illegally. You don't have a record." He didn't want his workers to have problems. If a worker got into trouble, he fired them. He was religious and wanted things to be correct. He said nothing will happen; nothing will happen. We went to jail. Because we had just come in to work, none of us had eaten lunch. We got to the jail about five in the evening. They took our pictures, put us in a cell. We said we that were hungry, that we hadn't eaten. They said that they'd give us something to eat. And so some began to be afraid.

I had friends who still had debts, and those in debt were worried. They were still paying them. They said, "What am I going to do?" Especially a man from Michuacan, Mexico. He was crying. He said, "They are going to kill me."

"No, no, they won't kill you. We will get out of here, because the patrón said he would pay." He said, "I will pay money so that you can get out."

We said to the man, "Don't cry. Don't be sad. Everything will be all right."

"No, they will kill me," he said. "I have a debt. And if I return now without that money, with all the violence, they will kill my family and me."

"It won't be like that; it won't be like that," we said. He was very sad, very angry.

The police put all of us in one cell. We saw a television program where it said that they had captured illegals, and that we'd been charged with three things: The first charge was for having false documents, the second for distributing false documents, and the third, for being in the country illegally. On the third day, the lawyer our patrón had sent told us that they were going to fine us $2,000. First, the lawyer said they'd pay $1,000, but then the fine went up. So the patrón paid $1,500 for each of us. We were in the county jail, but the judge said, "No, immigration wants them."

Eventually, the immigration came. They said, "You are going back to your countries." Some of us were very angry because we had been one month in jail. "You are going back to your countries because you are illegals; you have no right to be here." So we waited. Then they sent my companions and me to Alabama. We were in the Perry [County] prison for eight days. Then they sent us to Mississippi, then Louisiana. But before, when we left the jail in Pensacola, my $800 wasn't $800 anymore. I said, "I had $800. What happened to it?"

"Here you have to pay for your accommodation. You have to pay for your food." Of the $800, they only gave me $450.

"But why me, and the others no?"

"Because the others didn't have money."

Later they told me, "You are going to go; they're going to deport you." When they sent us to the federal prison, we really knew we would be deported.

In Oakdale, Louisiana, when it was my turn to go before the judge, she said to me, "Why are you here?"

And so I, a little angry, said, "Like you don't know why we are here?"

"No, no, tell me; why are you here?"

"In the first place, I am a Guatemalan. I live in a country where there are many problems, where there aren't any opportunities, where people are assassinated at any time, a place where there is no employment, a place where at times, you die of hunger. It's a place where if you plant a little, your products have no value, a place that has nothing to give us." The judge didn't say anything. The interpreter repeated what I had said. After fifteen minutes, the judge asked if I had an ID to return to Florida? I said yes.

"Do you have money to pay for a bus from here to Florida?" I said I did. From the $800, I had $450, but I had spent about $50 in the jail. So I still had $400. I could take a bus from Louisiana to Florida. I thought it would cost about $50. I said I had enough to return.

"What would you do?"

"Work in the restaurant."

"Can someone receive you in Florida?"

"Yes."

"Who?"

"My boss, my patrón."

"And do you have an ID?"

In my wallet I had an ID. "Yes, I have an ID."

"All right, then you can go to Florida."

There was someone—I don't know who it was—the prosecutor for the government. He rose up. "No," he said, "this man can't go back to Florida. This man is going to be deported. The government has found this man guilty of four things."

"And what are those four things?"

"Possessing false documents, distributing false documents (which was not true), being illegally in the United States, and conspiracy against the United States." How can all that be? We were only working. Our crime was to work. It had nothing to do with us trying to harm anyone. That never happened. Never. I had made friends . . . . I had two friends who were police in Atlanta. We always greeted each other on sight when they weren't on duty. My friends, the young students there, it never occurred to me to harm anyone. They had said, "conspiracy." In the end, I understood why they did it like that. All of us who were deported were charged with those four things.

I have many companions who hate the United States. Me, I don't, because, as I said, that country gave me the means to buy my land; that country gave me the means to build my house; that country made me reflect on other things. There are many good things there that we don't do here, things I want us to do here. For example, the collection of the garbage, the treatment of waste. The punctuality that the people have. To arrive five minutes late is not good. Here, we must be punctual. That is what I am teaching my children.

There were also people who want to do harm, but those who want to do harm are about 3 percent. In the United States, there are many good people. This must be recognized. I knew many people, many who were advanced in age. They always greeted you. Our American neighbors always invited us to their parties

My intention was to do my thesis. But I couldn't do it. I bought the land that I have here with the money I made there in the U.S. And I was able to build my house. It wasn't much, but I was able to do that.

When I was a refugee in Mexico, I thought about things that had happened when the army persecuted us. When I returned to Guatemala, I was still thinking about those things. I thought about the war all the time . . . the war. At times, when I got together with friends, we said we never had a childhood like those who are children now. Children now have more possibilities. They aren't thinking that at any moment, the army will kill them or hunt them down, or that at any moment, they will have to flee to another place. "We have to go. The enemy is here." The army was our enemy. I had those things in my head. When I got to Guatemala, I couldn't get them out.

At the time of our return, there were many observers accompanying us. They were from the United States, from Canada, Spain, Germany, France, Denmark, from many countries. I met one I'll never forget. He was young. His name was Bill. This man, Bill, said to me, "Poetry is so beautiful." He carried a book by Miguel Angel Asturias. I love poetry. I asked him, "What is poetry for you?"

He said, "Poetry is what you are. It's what your eyes can see. It's what your heart feels. It's what you think. That is poetry."

"What you feel?"

"Yes, what you feel. History, the life that we have. That is poetry." I began to write some things. At the age when the youngsters begin to write, they write *amorias,* love poems, the things you write for your *novia* [girlfriend]. I began to write them. Then I wrote a poem for Mayalan. Someone told me, "That poem you just wrote for Mayalan, in time that could be the hymn to Mayalan."

"I doubt it. Don't exaggerate. It's just a poem." I kept writing and writing.

I had watched my companions in the United States. Some of them were young . . . . They were young, but they were doing well.

I had friends who had left their families in Guatemala or in Mexico. They suffered very much because they were always worried, "What could be happening with the family?" They said, "Now that I am eating well, what is happening with my family?" And so I decided to write about that. The material I wrote was left in Florida.

I wrote a story that is called, *Cuento de un Amor,* Story of a Love. Others have said why don't you change the name. *Cuento de un Amor* isn't something that grabs your attention. Give it another name. "No," I said. "That's it. I want it to be named that." I write a bit about a young man who has left his family here in Guatemala. But when he gets to the United States, he doesn't find work. His wife and his son are dying of hunger in Guatemala. He keeps on working, keeps on struggling. He earns some dollars and sends it to them. But it's not enough. He continues for five months, suffering. He hasn't found anyone to give him work. He keeps trying and trying, calling his family and saying, "Look, things will change. I'm here in a place where many say there is opportunity, but at times, it's not as they paint it. There are people who are poor, people who suffer." For a year, it continued the same. The debts were mounting. He loved his family, but after the passage of time, he was completely lost. He lost his family, he lost his children, he lost many things. He kept working, working. He took up vices, drank beer, took drugs, got into an accident with his car. But then life in the States gave him hope again; it gave him something.

He started a new family. He returned to Guatemala with the family he made with another Guatemalan. When they arrive here, his children are dead, and his wife as well. They owed large debts. The woman went crazy, and that killed her.

Now I have some education. I'm a teacher. This year, I will finish my studies in the university. I have been the coordinator of the Organization of Schools in Solidarity of Ixcán since 2009. The organization is now well established. We have projects in association with the University of Valencia. We've given grants to ten communities of Ixcán. I have projects, for example, in Cuarto Pueblo, where there is now a school kitchen. We're going to build a kitchen and cinderblock latrines in Las Mojadas. We're setting up gardens in ten schools.

Our idea is to change this community, to change this country. Those of us who are here must work, not have an outsider come and say to us, "This is what you need to do." No, it will come from ourselves. The change will begin here with us.

I'm very happy to be working with the Northwest Educators Association. Now I am going to finish my studies. When I began to work in the association, they said, "You are going to study. You have completed your sociology courses. Now do your thesis; we will pay for it."

I said "Very well, thank you for the opportunity."

In the United States I had made contacts because I wanted to study, to finish. I renewed the contacts, and they called saying I could do my thesis with Atlantic International University. Their headquarters are in Honolulu. When I called to register, they told me that there was one in Guatemala. I have to complete a hundred fifty credits, as well as my thesis.

The university has validated all my experiences. They have given me credit for my poetry, for the courses in sociology I'd taken before, the writings I've done, and the projects I have completed. I'm studying by correspondence on the internet. So with a bit of luck, I will graduate on the fourth of December.

Jesús Camposeco Ross
Colonia 15 Octubre,
La Trinidad Esquintla,
February 5, 2011

I n 1969, I arrived in Ixcán. Mayalan was not yet established. The base of the co-operative was in the First Center. There we were attended by Padre Guillermo Woods. We solicited entry into the co-op, and prepared the land for the arrival of the family. First, we planted milpa. Later, when there were corn and

Jesús Camposeco Ross

beans, we brought the family from Santa Ana Huista, from the aldea Buena Vista. We were eight families.

I went with my family, my younger children. Patricia was about nine years old, another younger one was about six. They walked from Barillas to Ixcán, because we carried the cargo. When Mayalan was formed, that is where we were affiliated with the co-operative. They gave us a parcela of four hundred cuerdas [about twenty-eight acres]. We were content working there. It was a good life. For us, a piece of land like that was a lot. Everything was going fine, each with their customs and music. I remem-ber one person we called "Juan Violón." His name is Juan Quiñones. He was bitten by a snake and lost his leg. In those days, he played *violón* with the marimba, so we called him "Juan Violón."

We heard about the problems caused by the army in Xalbal. . . . Then they came to Mayalan. The situation of the people was falling apart; there was a lot of fear. We stayed on for a long time, but there arrived a moment when we couldn't withstand what was happening. On the part of the army, it was fierce. We couldn't live there, and so we went to the jungle. There was no alternative, and for our compañeros, it was the same.

Things became more serious, so I decided to leave the family and join the guerrillas. It was a difficult situation. They didn't know exactly where I had gone. Just like that, I left my family, left my children. The oldest ones were working in the parcela.

Many left like that. We felt the army would persecute us because we were in a co-operative. According to them, if you were in a co-operative, you were a guerrilla. You were against the government. It wasn't true, but that is what the army thought, and so they persecuted us. Some of us were able to get out, leaving the family. It was a sacrifice.

The army took over. They built their fort, and they began to harass my family. The family had to leave for a time. My wife and my children went to our pueblo, Santa Ana Huista, because their grandparents were there. There were other families there, but in reality, no one to care for them. During the regime of Rios Montt, the situation got more complicated. There was the scorched earth policy. People were pressured to be against one another, neighbor against neighbor. People became divided.

From Santa Ana, the family left for Chiapas, Mexico. They didn't come through Ixcán but went by way of Dolores and Comalapa. There was army on the border, but they crossed in the night. My mother told me how they crossed. The parcela was abandoned.

And so I decided to stay in the jungle for as long as necessary. I was fourteen or fifteen years in the jungle.

For those living in Mexico, everything changed. The women stopped wearing their *corte*. They were traditional, but they changed out of fear because the army came after them again and again. However, my mother said, "I'm not going to change my corte. They can kill me, but I won't change my traditional dress." And, years later, that was how we buried her.

My mother didn't know where I was for twelve years. She knew nothing about me. She was in Mexico many years. When I finally went to visit her, she said, "Who are you?" When I told her, she fainted.

In the war, I lost a son. His name was Jubilio, Jubilio Camposeco Leyba. He was going to Ixcán. He decided . . . he didn't go armed. He ran into the army. They killed him there in Quiche. We never learned more about him.

When the cease-fire was signed I was in Comalapa, in the state of Chiapas, with my mother. I was trying to see how I could return to Guatemala, to get back the parcela.

Many were in agreement with those of us who were in the guerrillas. But many, a good part, were not. So to avoid problems, I didn't return to the co-operative. They accepted my son, Orlando, who was in Chiapas, but he couldn't withstand the situation there. . . . He returned to Mexico. Now he is in San Cristobal.

Another of my sons wanted to go to Ixcán, but they didn't accept him. He didn't come for over a year, so they rejected him. He had to have been there, doing collective work, and other things. So we lost the parcela.

Here in La Trinidad, we have no more than fifty cuerdas [about three and a half acres] for each family. Some can make it, working hard. It's coffee land. But for those with large families, it is difficult, yes, a bit difficult.

I went into the jungle with the guerrillas because I thought that . . . the struggle would cause a change in the country right away. One had to do something, because we could not live as we were. There was no peace. There was no "life." The family was afraid. "Let us make a change." I looked at the situation, knowing the situation of the poverty, knowing how the people lived, poor people, hard workers, honorable people, persecuted by the army. . . . "No, we must take another path. So with that thought, we went into the jungle, to struggle, to see if we could change our country.

Thinking back about whether it was worth it all, at this time, [I'd say] no, because in reality, we didn't achieve the objectives we desired, the changes. The situation continues to be nearly the same. If there had been an improvement . . . . But we can't say that we achieved our objectives. The peace accords and all that were signed. If everything that was agreed to had been honored, then yes, definitely yes. But . . . that is only a piece of paper. For us, the poor, there hasn't been sufficient compliance. The people are still suffering with hunger, malnourishment, injustice, all that. In our country, there is still not justice. The killings continue. Without a doubt, if some things had been achieved, if at least it had gotten better, if we could say our country had improved . . . but that hasn't happened yet.

I don't regret that I went, even though it was hard. Now, the struggle is different. It's not with arms. Now, the struggle is that one day, there is a government that is really for the people. But for the moment, we can't say that this exists.

I did what I could to better things. I continue the political struggle. But when one can't move . . . . For seven or eight years, I have not been well. One leg is shorter than the other. I can't do much, and they say I have leukemia. Look, at the moment I feel that I'm an invalid. But my uneasiness continues. One may die, but the knowledge of what needs to be done will never be lost. We won't lose that.

Patricia Camposeco Leiva
Colonia 15 Octubre,
La Trinidad Esquintla,
February 5, 2011

I arrived in Ixcán when I was about six years old. What I remember of the Ixcán is the jungle. Pure jungle. I remember it was a very long journey from the place where we lived, Buena Vista, in Huehuetenango. We had to travel partly on foot and partly by bus. It took many days to get to Mayalan. There were few houses.

Patricia Camposeco Leiva

My father began to work together with other friends in the place where he was going to build a small house with wood walls and a roof thatched with leaves they cut in the jungle. It was very mountainous. You couldn't see anything but rivers, birds, animals, wild animals. I remember the cries of the wild animals.

The place wasn't very populated. Later, like two years after we arrived, there were more houses, and Mayalan was taking shape. There were houses here and there.

When the violence began, we went to Santa Ana Huista, to Buena Vista, the place we came from. My father was not with us, just my mother and my younger brothers and sisters. My older brother didn't come with us either. But we just stayed for a while and then returned to Ixcán.

In Ixcán, we went to live at the parcela where there was a small house. It was in Center Estrellita. We heard from Mayalan and other surrounding centers that the army was approaching. Dead people were starting to appear in various places. That made us begin to worry, because it was said they were searching for people who collaborated with the guerrillas. We were advised that the army was coming to the place where we lived. So we were able to leave the house in time, and we were far away when we saw that the army had come to the house to record everything that was there. We left, but we didn't go to the aldea, Buena Vista. We went to the border.

I decided to help my mother cross the border with the aid of an uncle. We went to a place called Guadalupe Victoria, in Chiapas, Mexico. We were there only a short while. I didn't like it. I missed our house. I missed the place we were from. So I told my mother that I would return to look for my father and brother. I was in Comitan a while. After some months had passed, I came again to Ixcán.

The violence had increased very much. There were many dead, everywhere in the pathways. It wasn't possible to live in the houses. It was necessary to sleep in the jungle. When I arrived in the CPR, many of the people in Ixcán were dying in the jungle. They were trying to hide, fleeing from the army. I decided to stay with them, and contacted the guerrillas. I joined with them, and there I remained. I was thirteen or fourteen years old. I was not yet "aware." My awareness came later, from the roots of what I'd seen in the area.

How was it possible that there were so many dead, and that the army killed them, the campesinos. I remembered that there was a large co-operative, and that my father was a strong participant, a very active community leader. Together with other groups, he helped his people very much.

I didn't understand the magnitude of the problem—why the army had come there to kill so many people I knew. The majority who lived there had emigrated from various places. For example, we were part of a large group who came from the aldeas of San Antonio, Buena Vista, Santa Ana Huista. Groups also came from Huehuetenango, the Canjobales, the Mam, and all lived supposedly in harmony in Ixcán, no? But when the repression began, all that changed. That made me follow in the footsteps of my father. He was the first who joined the struggle. I stayed there for sixteen years, until the peace accord was signed.

[When the peace accords were signed], I was in the camp of the demobilized, in Mayalan. There we turned in our arms to the institutions that were represented there. We turned in all we had. They signed the peace accord on December 29, 1996. About two months before that, we turned in the arms.

I think the policy of the directors at the head of the revolutionary movement was not the best. Maybe it could have been done in a better way. There were many people who came at the end only to fill their cup. There had to be a determined number of people from the guerrillas to turn over everything at the signing of the peace, Not everyone came. At that moment, the revolutionary movement had become much weaker. Many people weren't there. Many weren't in agreement with continuing the struggle. They had left the jungle.

Since many of the guerrillas had gone back to their families, there weren't enough when they were turning in their arms at the ceremony, so they created a policy of bringing in many people from the city, people who had collaborated in some form with the guerrillas.

What pained me was that those people ended up benefiting most from the projects that were established by the URNG. I saw for myself that they received things like housing projects. There were people who got good houses even though they were only a couple of days in the jungle. Those people were the ones who benefited. There were many comrades in the war who lost their families, who were left orphans, who lost their land, who lost everything. What about all the combatants, and all the friends who were there at the front, like cannon fodder? What happened to them? They got nothing. Only a few, a very few, received benefits.

To come out of the jungle after living a life of struggle . . . to come out into the legal world . . . without education. When the schools were formed and I had an opportunity to study, the repression started. So I never had a chance to study. For me, the guerrillas were my school. That is where I learned what I know.

I was always with the guerrillas, in communication with the CPR. Yes, there was always coordination with them. After the signing of the peace treaty, there was a program to finish grade school in one year, middle school in one year, and high school in one year. I got into that program and was able to receive my high school diploma at the University of San Carlos, here in the capital. That's how I was able to get my diploma.

But in reality, what has helped me was what I learned during the war. That is where I learned to read and write, with charcoal and a piece of board.

After the signing of the peace accord, we felt like mute people, with our arms crossed as if there was nothing much to do. We couldn't find work. One would ask for work, but they asked for papers, they asked, "What is your profession?" It was complicated because the only thing we knew was the use of arms. So we had many difficulties.

Also, I was with a small girl. When I was in the jungle, I had a baby, a girl. She is now twenty-two years old

When she got out of school here, she said she would go to the university. Later, she began to say there was a possibility of going to

Cuba. I never thought that could happen. Since I didn't show much interest, she began pushing things herself. She went to the embassy and began to make inquiries, to arrange for papers. She got a grant to study medicine in Cuba. I didn't believe it. I thought it wasn't true. And truthfully, when she told me she was going to Cuba, I was nearly sick. I hadn't lived with her for long. Because I was in the guerrillas, I had left her with families in Mexico since she was a baby. When she was eight, she came to live with me. It was hard for us. After so much time not living together, we didn't feel close to each other. It was as though she never forgave me for having left her. When she said that she was going to Cuba, I felt very sad because we had begun to live well together. Now she says that Cuba has helped her a lot to understand that entire situation. And she finally appreciates . . . appreciates everything. Her name is Sylvia, Sylvia Patricia.

I can't bring her home each year for lack of money. We have had many economic problems because of the health of my father, the health of my mother, and now my baby also has some problems. Sylvia has been in Cuba four years and has come to see me twice.

The grant is for six years; two years remain. Her vacations are in July, and she can come for one month to Guatemala. I still don't know if I am able to save the money. If there are not more problems with my father's health, or my mother's, then, yes, she could come. The ticket is expensive, and also her room and board there. The grant is good. Still, I have to help her monthly to buy the things she needs. But I am happy that she is there.

So it was very hard for me because I couldn't find work. It was very difficult. But later, with the passing of the years, one adapts to this form of life. Now I work with a foundation that promotes psycho-social aid to families who were victims of the conflict. I like my work very much. The people appreciate me, and I'm grateful for that. The work is good. We look for help for those families. They have one or two or three family members who were "disappeared." And they live in so much poverty. My job is in the area of Santa Lucia, Cotzumalguapa, on the coast, in the direction of Mazatenango. I'm working there now. I am forty-three.

Juan Juarez Juan
Pueblo Nuevo, February 12, 2011

The Kekchi say that Ixcán . . . . "Ix" is the feminine, "can" is a snake, so a female snake. But the word wasn't born there. It came from the Kanjobales. In Kanjobal, the name is not Ixcán but "Yichcan," meaning the end of the highlands. In the old days, our fathers, looking out over the great jungle from Santa Eulalia, said that the sky and the land ended here: "Yichcan" or "Ichk'an." Yichcan has the significance that the sky falls [to meet] the earth. The end of the *alto,* the highlands. That is what they thought. It was the edge of the earth. So they named it Ichk'an.

My name is Juan Juarez Juan. Juan is my given name, Juarez for my father, and Juan for my mother.

I am sixty-one years old. I live here in Pueblo Nuevo, Ixcán. I'm originally from the municipality of Santa Eulalia, Huehuetenango.

I was twenty-two years old when I arrived here in Ixcán, in February 1975, with my wife and two children; one was a year and a half old, the other three months. Thanks be to God, that all of my six children, four born here in Ixcán, are still alive. We are grandparents of thirteen grandchildren. There are three daughters-in-law.

My life before was working in the fincas, the coffee farms in the area of Mazatenango. I began going with my father and my three older brothers when I was twelve years old. We lived in extreme poverty because we had no land, nor was there work. In those days, it was thought that the fincas of coffee, cane, and cotton were where one could make some money. We gave our labor for a miserable salary. We worked for nothing, but we did it because there was no alternative. I made forty cents a day. The adults made fifty cents. Later, the salaries went up. The adults began to make sixty cents a day. My job was to water and fertilize the small coffee seedlings and weed the plots of coffee trees. That was the work for us, the adolescents. The women and girls would weed and fertilize. They made thirty cents a day.

That was the only work available at that time, making those thirty or forty cents a day. We felt we were at least making a bit of money. We put the centavos together to help our parents, or to be able to buy some clothes. That was what I was doing at age twelve: Go to the fincas, return to my pueblo, stay at home for four or five months, return again for the coffee harvest.

My wife also grew up in the fincas. We were in the same situation. When we were eighteen, we got together and had two children. We were reliving the experience of our fathers. After working for so many years, they didn't have anything, just giving away their labor for the finqueros. I was familiar only with the bill of one quetzal. The bills of five, ten, or the bill of twenty quetzales, I didn't know.

We got the idea to look for some land, a place to live, and to make a life with our children. The Catholic church gave out information in the Masses that in the Ixcán, there was land for those who wanted to go there. That made us wake up and think of coming to Ixcán. We decided, my wife and I, to come, although my parents and her parents didn't agree with us. They complained because they thought we would abandon them completely.

Ixcán was known to be a jungle, a distant place that was hard to get to. They never thought that one day, they could come and visit us. That is how they saw it. But in February of 1975, we decided to walk from Barillas until we arrived in Ixcán. We found a happy life, although in the beginning, it was very difficult because we had no money. My family arrived with thirty quetzales that we brought from the highlands. It lasted six months. When we had spent it, we

Juan Juarez Juan

had nothing left. We were without money for milk for the children. It was very difficult for us, but we managed to survive. Later, when we harvested our milpa, we had corn and beans. And so our situation regarding food changed. But we could survive despite all those problems of scarce resources.

We got a parcela, then we began to plant a bit of coffee, a bit of cardamom. I didn't have difficult problems because of my experience in the fincas. I harvested my coffee and cardamom, even if it was just a little. And so I got to know the bills of fifty quetzales; I got to know the bills of one hundred quetzales. In 1977, 1978, I didn't have much money, but I wasn't in the difficult situation as before.

And also, something very important that I want to recount: How did I get to Ixcán? Through the help of the church. Not only through the church but through the help of Padre Woods, may he rest in peace. He did the work. What caught my attention was that as a foreigner, he did the work that a Guatemalan should have done. A foreigner shouldn't have needed to come and struggle for the land.

I have many memories of the great work that Padre Guillermo did. He fought for about a thousand associates of the co-operative of Ixcán Grande. We each got a parcela of four hundred cuerdas. And within this co-operative, there were five communities: Mayalan, Xalbal, Pueblo Nuevo, Cuarto Pueblo, and Los Angeles. I was adding up the quantity of land from the Rio Ixcán to the Rio Xalbal, approximately six hundred eighty *caballerías*, which is to say six hundred eighty thousand cuerdas, a great extension of lands . . . for a large number of people. Here in Pueblo Nuevo, there are various Mayan languages: Kanjobal, Jacalteco, Popti, Chuj, Mam, Ixil, Kachiquel. There are also families that don't speak any Mayan language, just Spanish.

And so the great coming together that we had here in those days was an example of the unity of the struggle in the co-operatives. Everyone was helping together. Padre Guillermo and the directors were guiding the co-operative. It was an achievement for us. We became "conscious." That consciousness, that awareness, was what united us with someone of good will to work for the general good, not for our personal interests. That led to the idea that, yes *we* can do things.

In the '80s, after the death of Padre Guillermo, the repression of the army began. We don't think his death was just an accident but that it was provoked by certain people because of the help he was giving to the campesinos. It led us to think that there are persons who don't want a particular person or the church to work for the good of the indigenous people. And so the repression began with the purpose of suppressing us, the co-operative members, because we were organized, struggling together. We were represented by a co-operative with the idea to export our products to foreign countries. But when the war came, the result was that everything came to a halt.

There was a guerrilla movement fighting for a revolutionary government in which the people would make the decisions, a government in which everyone would live in equality. Those were the terms that the guerrillas were demanding in those years—all in contrast to those who were then governing [the country]. This provoked the army to come here to Ixcán and build their military forts in all the villages, with the aim of controlling the people, to repress and intimidate the population.

Meanwhile, the guerrillas were growing as a result of all the injustices being done by the government on the national level, the repression, the disappearances of leaders. In the 1980s, the repression grew stronger. The well-known massacre here in Ixcán, in Cuarto Pueblo, occurred on October 14, 1982, during the government of Lucas Garcia. Next, Rios Montt came to power, and it got worse. We went into the jungle with the hope that the repression would end, but it got worse and worse. And so we went to seek refuge in Mexico.

The Mexican government didn't want to recognize us with refugee status. They treated us as economic migrants, but that was not true. We went to Mexico to seek refuge. We were victims of a civil war, of a scorched earth [policy] that unfolded in those years.

When we arrived in Mexico, our situation changed. We had security for our families, thanks to the Catholic Church, the Committee of Christian Solidarity, and the United Nations, who were all very dependable. The presence of the High Commission of the United Nations, the pressure from the church, from the Mexican indigenous organizations, and other organizations that were in solidarity with us all helped a lot. They petitioned the government to give us legal recognition as Guatemalan refugees in Mexico.

And that is what came to pass. We were in Mexico for thirteen years. During those thirteen years of pain and sadness, we were helped by having a school. We learned to organize ourselves even more, into groups that included men, women, elders, and the young. Everyone organized. We initiated the struggle for a return to Guatemala. In order to initiate a process of negotiation with the government, we named representatives. We presented certain conditions, how we wanted to make the return to our country with dignity. We demanded security in the places to which we were planning to return. And that is what came to be.

When those from the land reform projects of INTA returned, the sad part was that they had no legal documents regarding their land titles. So while the land was left abandoned, the government had given the land to other campesinos. There were places where people got back their land, and places where others were occupying the land.

In our case, the co-operative members in 1976, with the help of the Catholic Church, had received the general land title through the Diocese of Huehuetenango. That served us as a legal basis to defend our land. Although the government had brought people from the west, from the south coast, and from other places to populate the area of the co-operatives, with the documents granted in 1976, we were able to recover our land. And so we came again, to repopulate the Ixcán. We returned in October 1993. In 1995, the returns ended. Some had returned, but another group of members of the co-operative stayed in Mexico. The truth is that we didn't all return to our country.

What I understand, as I was a representative of the refugees in Mexico, according to the census taken by the United Nations High Commission for Refugees, we were forty-five thousand Guatemalan refugees in the three states of Chiapas, Quintana Roo, and Campeche. Those of us who did finally return were about twenty-five thousand. So about twenty thousand Guatemalans stayed in Mexico. But here in the co-operative of Ixcán Grande, counting approximately fifteen hundred members, I understand that of those, there were three hundred fifty parcelas whose owners didn't return. Among those, there could have been some who had died. So there were about two hundred twenty-five free parcelas, and those were given to the sons of our families.

In our communities, from the unity that we had in those days before we left to live in Mexico, we learned many good things. After the return, divisions opened among ourselves. The divisions came from what? They were born from within ourselves. When we arrived here, some families were divided in ideology and politics. Some recognized the difficult situation we were in, that we were suffering. So we continued with a principled struggle against injustice. But part of the people believed that we had been tricked, that we didn't live in a situation of injustice—as though we went into exile because someone had planted in us an idea, a mistaken ideology, and that now after the return, our country was all right. They took advantage of political divisions to get power for themselves.

Certain persons offered themselves up as agents for political parties, convincing the people that the guerrillas were the ones who'd tricked us so we'd be forced into exile, as if in our country, there had been a change. But it was not true, and so the politics began. We went into exile during the times of Lucas Garcia and Rios Montt, and when we returned, Rios Montt had organized his political party, the FRG. There were groups of people among us that were helping the FRG, the very ones who drove us out.

In the case of Pueblo Nuevo, we were divided into eight sections by eight different political parties. And this weakened our community, weakened our co-operative. When we began to reorganize our co-operative, we weren't operating with a clear consciousness but with confused thinking. The divisions began; clashes of ideas began; we didn't agree.

At the national level, the situation in our country was more and more difficult for the people who never went into exile, the people who stayed, who were in the civil patrols. The government had made a promise to the ex-civil patrol. Their complaint was that they had collaborated [with the government] in the time of civil war. They'd done everything that the army demanded, and afterward, they were not acknowledged. They saw that those of the URNG had turned in their arms, and that there was small help given to the ex-combatants. This gave the ex-patrollers the idea that, "We suffered, but they didn't give us anything." And so began this conflict. It was on a national level, and there were so many ex-patrollers. They argued that the government hadn't complied to pay the few cents they'd offered.

We that went into exile learned many good things. We organized ourselves. We don't believe that our country is reformed. Within the five communities of Ixcán Grande, there are divisions. There is no community where there are not divisions by political party. That is what I see now. We are in a very difficult time.

I am clear that I came back to Guatemala for my land, for my family. We returned with the idea that we would continue struggling. We understand that the situation in the country is not easy, even though there are some who think that the situation has improved. But that is not certain.

The younger ones have a point. They didn't know the realities that existed when we went into exile. They only heard stories about what had happened. They grew up in Mexico with more freedom, and then returned to a different life. Many see that the Guatemalan situation is difficult, but since they have Mexican papers, men and women, they prefer to go to Mexico. It's better for them to go to Cancún, or to Campeche, places where they say there is work. Then they can make something of themselves, make a life—not the best but at least have some money, and receive a salary every fifteen days.

Others don't want anything. They just exist, looking for what to do. If they take a good path, it is at least there for them. But if they detour . . . . One of the problems that most affects us here is alcohol. Many youngsters fall into alcoholism.

Also there is a migration to the United States and to Mexico. Because of the scarcity of economic resources, they go to the United States or to Cancún to make money.

Persons who go to the United States . . . . If they go with the idea, and don't forget it, of making a small savings with their low salary, then they can do something with the money they make. But if they lose control, the little they make is not enough. If they overspend, the vices and debility are not far away. A person can lose everything. It's the same with the women. The women go, the single ones. But what happens? In a while, they are single mothers with a baby they can't support. It is not easy for them. This is a difficult problem.

I have two sons who are in the North. One is the father of a family. At least he has communication with his wife. I also have a single son who is in the United States. He is now more than thirty years old. He too communicates with us. He helps us, always sending us some money. We don't receive large amounts from him, but at least there's communication. He has known how to control the vices, and so he's not falling into that. But he has told us about the many people he has seen there, that the little they make weekly is not enough. They have forgotten their families, even though they have children. They don't send anything to their families. The family here is suffering, and the children who remained behind need to see their father. They need the help of a father, but they don't receive it. They have problems as a result. They can't study or go to school. They want to continue studying, but can't because they need money.

Here in Ixcán, in the case of Pueblo Nuevo, we have 583 owners of parcelas. Taking into account the sons who are not landowners but have families, this community has between nine hundred and a thousand families. It is the biggest village in Ixcán. When I was doing a study with Padre Ricardo Falla about migrants, we discovered there were about a hundred twenty-five persons from Pueblo Nuevo who were in the North.

Mirna Castellanos de Hollstegge
San Juan Sacatapecez, February 6, 2011

I had forgotten this thing that happened in Ixcán. We were living in La Resurección, Tercer Pueblo. There was a general assembly [of the co-operatives]. Rolando Lopez was there, along with Miguel TePaz, Bill Woods, David, and me. When we were in the reunion, the army surrounded the church. We left and went up to our house. It was above, on a small hill. We were sitting there when the firing began. I think it was the first time there had been shooting.

Rolando, the padre, and the men ran out. We women stayed in the house. When the soldiers started firing, there was a riot. The campesinos grabbed some of the soldiers and took their weapons. No one was killed, but in the confusion, when the people began to run, someone grabbed the weapons. When the men came back up to the house, they told us what had happened.

The soldiers were from the fort in Xalbal. They had taken the health aide hostage. The commander said that if the weapons weren't returned, they would kill the health aide.

I remember this very well. Bill and Dave went to talk to the people, and said to them, "You have to return the arms. When a soldier loses his weapon, it is the worst thing that can happen to him. You have to give back the guns, [or they will kill the health aide]. The co-operative members discussed it, and finally they gave over the rifles.

Mirna Castellanos de Hollstegge

Bill said, "David and I will go turn over the arms." I remember this as if it were today. Bill getting in the plane with Dave and the guns. . . . They went to Xalbal, and there they exchanged the arms for the health aide. I can't remember his name, but I think it was Gonzalo, Gonzalo Ross.

Gonzalo Ross Hernández
Jacaltenango, November 25. 2011

My name is Gonzalo Ross Hernández. I was born in a *cantón* of Jacaltenango, Cantón Pila, they say there.

I didn't go to school. I wanted to, but my father said those who went to school were children of the rich. They have clothes they bought, uniforms for the Fifteenth of September, and we didn't have the money for that. He didn't have land. In those days, there was municipal land that one could use, but as we were many in the family . . . the women . . . . It's a question of culture . . . . The women stayed in the house, and it was the man who supported the family. My father lived by working as a day laborer. If he worked, he made some money. If he didn't get work, he looked elsewhere. Here, the people are at different economic levels. Some go through life very favorably. Others, like my parents and me, are day laborers. If we get work the day that dawns, we eat; if not, then no. So growing up, I couldn't go to school.

In those days, the army took people; they called it the "*cupo*." They grabbed the young men. They didn't ask if one wanted to go or not; they just nabbed them and made them do military service. I had always lived here. I felt like I was blindfolded, like I hadn't experienced anything. I wanted to know something more. Before my seventeenth birthday—I was sixteen plus a few months—I heard they were taking boys. I went out so they would take me. At least I would get out of Jacal. So they took me as part of the cupo.

I was stationed in Quiche, which at that time was the Sixth Military Zone. I was there for two years. Marco Antonio Sosa was an officer there. He was the commander of a mortar squad. I knew him very well.

I was there when they were discovered. We were told that something was wrong, that a captain based in Totonicapan . . . . On the base, the order was given that anyone entering the base suspiciously in the night was suspect. We were to challenge them three times, then shoot.

He came . . . . Since he was based in Totonicapan, he entered on the highway that comes from Xela to Quiche. There was a bridge just before the base. He got out, leaving his car at the bridge. He walked across another small bridge in front of the base's wall. The soldier on guard challenged him, but the captain didn't respond. The soldier charged his rifle, and challenged him again. If he didn't do something, the soldier was going to shoot. I knew him. He was my captain. We called him Captain Churro. He didn't answer the challenge but walked back down, got in his car and left.

The soldier reported what happened. In the morning, they sent for the captain. I don't know if he was the one who said that there was some plan, a coup, or something. There were six officers from the Sixth Zone. I remember that among them was Jon Sosa, Captain Silva, Marco Antonio Martinez—he was a lieutenant colonel—and Gramajo, who later became minister of defense. The army sent them to the Cuartel General. Only Gramajo came back. I don't know if he was part of the coup, if they suspected him, or if he was an agent of the army itself, because later, he returned, but the others didn't.

They were under arrest for a month. I don't know if they had planned something. They escaped, and most of the soldiers from that base went with them. They killed the second in command, the commander of guard of the Cuartel General. They took heavy machinery, vehicles. That's when the guerrillas began. From there, it seems they went to Zacapa, to the base in Puerto Barios. They took everyone from that base, everyone. Tanks went. The only thing they didn't take were the airplanes.

And so the combat began. The army sent young pilots to bombard them. Instead of bombing the rebels, they bombed other areas.

Gonzalo Ross Hernández

They say that what Ydigoras, the president, did then was to send for retired pilots and had them bombard because the young ones wouldn't. That's when they began to harm the rebels, who dispersed. And so that is how Yon Sosa began. That's how I knew him.

Later, when I married, we left Jacal and went to Limonar. The only things I owned were a small hand bag, two lassos, a head strap, a machete, and a blanket, nothing more. The two of us went. I said, "Let's go, because if we stay here, I don't know what will happen. Here, it's much harder to find work than in the aldeas." I went to stay with my sister. I struggled to survive, to get a bit of corn. There, they paid with corn. They paid by the *mano*; each mano is five ears. They paid forty ears for a day of work.

I saved and bought wire. In those days, there was still land available. One could just get wire and fence in what one wanted. In that way, I got my piece of land. Later, I saw it was not good, that the land was poor. The better land had already been fenced in.

I grew up with some men who lived in La Laguna. I thought it might be better there, and so I went. I lived there seven years, also as a day laborer. At that time I was named an agricultural aide. There was no one else, so they elected me.

I began to go to the Project San José. That was where I met the priest who initiated the land reform project. He said that they had begun the project, and explained everything about it very well. He spoke of cardamom, of vanilla, and all that. He said that they were going to build houses, make streets, that they were going to create towns. And the cost . . . that the people should not be afraid of the cost.

Having nothing, working in the countryside, without hope … I was speechless at the proposal. "I am poor," I thought. "I don't have land here. I'm a day laborer." I thought it was the only opportunity I would ever have. They were still looking for the first ones to go to Ixcán.

If I had gone then, I would have been in the First Center, but I didn't go. My wife didn't want to, and I was still trying to find out what it was like there. Time went by. And so not until February 1972, after the assembly in Jacaltenango, did I go there. In March, I signed the contract for land with Victoriano.

When I was in La Laguna, after being the agricultural aide, they made me a health aide also. When I went to Ixcán, there were seventeen health aides. I didn't know them, but they said we should organize and that there should be a head coordinator in charge of the group. I was elected. I began to attend the courses in the hospital here in Jacaltenango. Besides the training as a health promoter aide, there was periodic upgrading as well as courses for the group coordinators. I was in Mayalan for about a year and a half. After that time, I got my parcela.

I don't know if you remember, Miguel, but I was the first to run the co-op store in Resurección. They built a small building on the edge of the runway, halfway down. David built it. He arranged for everything he needed there, agricultural implements, something to eat. Since I had worked some weeks in the store in Mayalan, he said to me, "I think you could work in Resurección if you want to. The only thing is, there are no people there. You will be alone."

"Well, why not?" I said, and went. The people who had already received a parcela nearby stayed in the jungle because they didn't have a house in town. During the day, people came, people from Mayalan and Xalbal. They were probationers who had contracted for land but still didn't have their parcela, and hadn't moved to the center of Resurección. Periodically, they came to take their turn at community work like improving the runway. And also, those who were clearing the jungle on their parcela came during the day. It was very lively. But in the night . . . silence everywhere. I was alone there.

There's something I'll never forget. I was there alone when the pilot Juan [Jon Stork] died [in a crash]. I wanted to speak to someone. There was no one. I was there alone, walking in circles on the runway, wanting to talk with someone. I remember that very well.

At last I went out to the parcela. It was Number 725. They named that area Center San Miguel. I worked there. I loved the people. It was something I hadn't felt before . . . .

I worked in the store when it was still attached to the clinic. I did the two jobs. I spent one month at a time on duty. Later, the store and the clinic were divided. There were those who only attended the sick, and those who took care of agricultural things. I and another were assigned to the clinic. We two took turns disbursing the medicine. The other man was José de León Diaz, from Santiago Chimaltenango. After we left Ixcán, I never saw him again. They say he is in Campeche.

I remember Ixcán. The beginning of the land reform project of colonization was very beautiful. The hope that one had to go and live there—it was worth the sacrifice. It was not the fault of those who began the project but the violence that changed things.

I wanted to be in school when I was little. I told you my parents were day laborers. What they earned in a day bought what they ate. And so I grew. I didn't have land. I didn't have an education. I went first to Limonar, then to La Laguna, and continued working as a day laborer. I was doing that when the notice arrived about the land project in Ixcán.

I felt that going there was the only chance for me. I was just beginning to better myself a bit. I wanted to plant and cultivate milpa. I planted coffee, I had ten cuerdas [about three-quarters of an acre] of bananas in the lower part of the parcela. I had planted six cuerdas of cardamom, and it was beginning to flower when the violence began. I didn't want to abandon it. If I returned here, what could I do? I didn't have savings. When I had to leave Ixcán, I left the only thing I had gained in my life. Everything ended.

I don't know if I told you this or not. I don't remember the date— I think it was the second fiesta of Resurección. In those days, the *ambulante,* the roving patrols of the military, were still around. They came from Xalbal in the evening. At about 6:30 p.m., I was hungry, so I went to the house. I hadn't had lunch, and now it was time for dinner. I was eating when I heard bursts of machine gun fire near the church.

Soon afterward, Padre Guillermo, Rolando López, and Miguel TePaz arrived. They told me, "Please don't go out; hide yourself. Don't return to the fiesta. The army is asking for you by name. It seems they want to capture you."

I stayed there for a time, but I decided to go. I couldn't hide forever. If they are looking for me, they will find me. Some day, they will come in the night. It's better that they see me, and that we find out what they want with me. Perhaps it would be safer to be with the people than to be alone. I returned to the assembly, but the army wasn't there. They had gone, but they took Noel Miguel. I heard that because they didn't find me, they took Noel. I supposed it was because I was treasurer of the co-operative. Maybe they thought I had money hidden, and they wanted to detain me and take the money.

But what happened? Why had they fired? You could see the bullet holes in the roof of the church. I didn't understand, because I was not involved in anything. One knows many things about one side or the other, but I preferred to be independent.

David, the padre, Miguel TePaz, and I, as members of the directors of the co-operative, were asking what had happened. It was learned that the people had taken the arms of one, or two . . . yes, two members of the military patrol. The army had fired because the people took two weapons. One got his rifle back, but the other did not.

We decided that to rescue Noel Miguel, we had to get back the weapon that had been taken. It must be someone we knew [who had the rifle], a parcelista. But who was it? We didn't know. So we sent out a message that in order to rescue Noel Miguel to please return the weapon—to turn it in or, if one didn't want to do it personally, to tell us where it was through a message. That's how it happened. A note came telling where the rifle was, and it was recovered. A commission went to Xalbal with the weapon to rescue Noel Miguel.

At first, the army denied it, saying that they hadn't taken anyone. But the people had seen it happen. "How can you deny that you kidnapped him when you took him from among all the people. We know he is here."

When the army realized that they couldn't deny it, they said, "Yes, he's here," and they would return him if it was true the commission had the arms. So there was an exchange. The army required the commission to sign a paper saying that Noel was healthy and that he hadn't been mistreated. But he was bruised everywhere. That's what I remember.

During the time when the violence was overwhelming, there wasn't yet a fort in Resureccion, and the guerrillas were mobilizing.

There was a generator to distribute electricity to the houses. The guerrillas cut all the electrical cables in front of everyone.

Five or six people a day left for Mexico. Soon, there were no more people; everyone had gone. When I saw that there was no one, I decided to go to the parcela. I had made a small shelter with wood shingles. It only needed to be closed in. We got there on a Saturday.

But I think they were watching me. Carmelino Luis came about 7 a.m. the first day we were in the house. He was an official of the guerrillas at that time. I had spoken to him about three times while he was a guerrilla, and I also knew him from before. He called me and said, "So you're here?"

"Yes," I said. "That's why I built this shelter."

"I don't know why," he said. "There are many people who are not aware of what is happening. We are at war. The army could come at any time. And for that reason, we are advising the people not to stay in their houses. Those who haven't gone into exile in Mexico, who want to stay here, have to form a camp." He didn't refer to the CPR, but that's what he meant.

I encountered the guerrillas about three times. The second time was when some of them came, called to me, and said that they wanted to talk with me. I knew them. One was the son of a parcelista from Mayalan. "So let's talk. We want to know if you are familiar with the movements of the army."

"Some things, yes, but only the most basic," I said. "Probably you know more because you are the ones who . . . . On the other hand, I just work on the farm."

They said, "But at least you know something. You must see something here. We don't believe that you don't know anything."

"Like what?" I said.

"People who have disappeared, who have been killed . . . ."

Miguel, do you remember Carmelino Recinos, the surveyor? He had "disappeared." The people said that he had gone to Barillas to visit his brother. And in mid-journey, nearing Mayalan, by the Río Ixcán, is where some said that he was killed. Others said that only his hand bag was found thrown on the path. Others, that the head was there but not the body. Others said the opposite, that the body was there. What do you think?

["I don't know," I answered. "I didn't see it. It could be true, or not. And as they say . . . ." That made him smile.]

They took me into the jungle, not very far. There was Carmelino. It was said that he was dead, that he'd been killed, but he had gone into the guerrillas. They told me that since I had served in the co-ops, it would be very good to consider fighting with them.

I said, "Well, I don't know. I think that it isn't necessary to be very intelligent to take up arms. Anyone can learn that. But I think I wasn't born for that. And I don't think it's because of fear. Why should I be afraid? What I think is that just as I don't want them to kill me, so I don't want to kill, to take someone's life. I respect the lives of others, so I'm not in agreement.

"Well then, what do you think about us?" they asked.

"Each one takes his own . . . path." I was considering what to say. I tried to be careful. I didn't know what they thought about me, but I tried to defend myself a little.

"So if you don't want to give us some information and don't want to join us either, at least give us something, a good suggestion that I can take back to them."

"Perhaps my suggestion is that each one work in his own way. For example, I work in health. I am a health aide. We also teach. We talk about why there are poor people, about the injustice; we talk about the exploitation and the malnourished children. All that I think is part of what you are doing. Only some don't use arms. Some made the decision not to take up arms. I think one has to respect people. Convince them, plant your ideas in them, but let them decide to accept your ideas or not. Don't trick them. That is my suggestion, that you respect the people even if they are illiterate. Don't lie to them." More or less, that's what I said to them.

After that, I never saw them for about a year and a half until Carmelino came and said I had to join the CPR. I went twice to meetings in the jungle, then returned to my family at our house. But later, I saw that everything was controlled. I couldn't speak freely in the talks there in the CPR. I remember they said that there had to be people guarding the camp. Some of those who were very involved with the guerrillas said that if we didn't leave, it was because we were the enemy or that we were informers for the army. And therefore, if we didn't join the guerrillas, we should do something to show we were not on the side of the army.

When I saw that the army was coming, they said I had to make a signal or fire a shot or light a firecracker or something. It occurred to me to say that that was bad. It was putting me in a trap. If one made a signal, lit a firecracker, the army would return and massacre them.

We still had not finished the meeting in the camp when they called me to speak to someone called Patricio. Who knows if that was his name? He said that I should never say that again, that all that was said there should not be contradicted. "And only because I know you, and because it's the first time, I'm not going to report you. I'm going to pardon you. I'm in charge, whoever contradicts . . . ."

I realized then that everything was controlled. I decided it was better neither to join the CPR nor to go to Mexico. They had everything planned, where everyone from Ixcán would go. I thought that if it is controlled here, it must be controlled in Mexico.

I've spoken about the guerrilla official Carmelino. He came to see me and told me that he had asked people before if they wanted to join the guerrillas or not. But now, the fighting was heavy. The situation was serious. He said that he who voluntarily accepts to join the guerrillas could then decide what he wanted to do. But he who decides not to had to leave, go into refuge in Mexico. And anyone who didn't go into exile, who stayed there, would be *ajustado*, killed, if they didn't cooperate.

They took me to a meeting, and obliged me to join them. . . . I saw I had no way out. If it was only me, I would have said what I thought, but I thought about my children and how I could protect them. So I asked them what options there were, what paths there were that I could commit myself to. Was there only one or what? What they had said when I'd seen them before was that I had to fight.

Now, they told me that there were three choices: one was to be a combatant, another was to be a member of a committee, and the third was to be part of an agricultural production group, plant milpa, corn, or whatever. It would be to supply the guerrillas. What I chose was to produce something, to work in agriculture. I saw that there was no way out. That was on a Sunday.

What tore my heart out was that when they obliged me to commit myself, I had to give information about all my family, not just myself. When I said I had two sons, they said, "Ah. Two soldiers more."

"What does that mean?" I asked. "That you will make of my sons what you want? Where is the just cause you talk about?" My sons were about six, six or seven years old.

In one of those meetings with the CPR there was another parcelista, Gaspar, who lived next to me. He also had two sons. He said, "*Señores,* I think that everything you are saying is good, but this about taking children without consulting their parents. I think that's not good. Two weeks ago, you took my sons, and I don't know where they are." Instead of listening to him, they called him out. I don't know what they said to him. I realized then that the people were not the owners of their own will. They were imposed upon.

That's what turned me away. I did not go to the other side, to Mexico. At that point, I decided to leave the little house on my parcela.

I knew there was an army fort, and that the guerrillas were also present. I knew there were many people who were not involved in anything but that the army accused them. The army saw them around, then accused them of being guerrillas, and they killed them. From whatever rumor, it would be said that someone must be "involved," then the army arrived and took them away. Anything could happen. That is what made me return to Jacaltenango—lies on the part of both sides.

I didn't want to leave there, but I decided it was better to return to Jacaltenango. We went to the parcela only to change and then went into the jungle. To one side of the parcela lived some paisanos who had a son involved with the guerrillas. Twice we saw him. I don't know if he was looking for us or just passing by. We were hidden in the tall grass, without food. We couldn't make a fire. We didn't have anything. We couldn't visit anyone. We were escaping from everyone, from the army, from the guerrillas, from the people. Where, where would we get things . . . food, anything? There was *palmito*, but it had to be cut, and cutting it made noise. We were more and more overcome by hunger. We drank a little water, but the water we were drinking became bitter . . . .

The children began to vomit after six days. I saw that we couldn't survive. On the seventh day, we decided to leave [the jungle]. We came out onto a pathway and circled around those who were controlling the area. We came out near Chipal, where Viviano had lived, close to Resurección. We could see smoke that was surely from an army camp. We thought perhaps they were in the town, so we returned into the fields and came out again in La Felicidad. There we stopped.

A man from San Sebastian Cuatán went to get ears of corn. He ground them in a mill and made something for us to eat and gave us coffee. We ate for the first time in seven days. I only ate half of it, and water, a bit of water. The next day, we made it to Mayalan. We had heard that there were no people there, but we encountered Tomas Pablo.

"Where are you going?" he asked.

"We're going to Barillas."

"Hay no!" he said. "They are going to kill you. They say they are going to close all the pathways."

We slept in the First Center. There, we talked with the owner of a dugout canoe, but he said he was not taking people across because he had been threatened not to continue doing it. Late at night, he arrived, "I will take you. I will take you across, but leave early so that no one sees you. I'll just check on the dugout, and return." We went down to the river, and he took us across. They say that two days later, they killed him and burned the dugout.

We went on by foot. Nothing happened. We didn't encounter anyone. At about 7 p.m., we got to Barillas. We were there two nights. Then we made it to Soloma. We also stayed there two nights. Everything was closed. There were barricades everywhere. We wanted to go directly to Jacaltenango, but we couldn't. We had to go from Barillas to Huehuetenango.

A man with a taxi said he was going directly to Huehue, but we only got as far as San Juan Ixcoy. There was a wire from one house to another. They said it was connected to a bomb so that cars couldn't pass. We returned, and the man left us in Soloma. We were there a week. After all that, we decided that somehow we'd get through from Soloma to Jacal, but we only got as far as Madrón where there was a big pine tree felled across the road. The driver said that the passengers should clear off the road, but the guerrillas were watching. So we went on foot to Topia. We were there two nights. Then a car came and brought us to Huehuetenango.

In Huehue, I met Juan Tebalán. He said, "You are lucky, Gonzalo, you are returning all together, not like me." He had gone to work in his parcela, and when he returned, he didn't find his family. Who knows what happened to them? If they were killed? His son disappeared and his wife and a daughter.

And so we came here to Jacaltenango, on the eighteenth of April 1982. We'd survived. No one had died.

When I came here, I was afraid, I was cautious. I remember Cruz Lopez. I think she was a nurse. She worked here in the hospital and was a good friend of Arnulfo, the priest. We knew each other since we had been in classes together. When I got here, she was the first to come and visit me. Later, she said that Arnulfo wanted to talk to me. He offered me a piece of land that belonged to the parish, and asked me if I wanted to work the land. I wouldn't have to pay rent. I could plant what I wanted. But I was afraid because people said that in that direction was where the guerrillas were. And so I said no.

The sisters at the hospital knew me because I had been to their courses and had worked as a health aide In June, I began to work with the program of health aides. I didn't go out into the countryside. We went to Huehue, to the towns, but not into the countryside. Later, when they signed the Peace Accords, I went freely into the country. That was the situation. It was very difficult. For now, I'm alive. Who knows when my turn will come?

Ixcán was our only hope. Four hundred cuerdas [about twenty-eight acres]. With that, a campesino, one who had never studied … . It was enough land to support oneself . . . . But it didn't happen. The land remained . . . .

Rosa Jiménez García
San Juan, Sacatepecez, February 6, 2011

Tigers, tigers, monkeys . . . . There was only jungle. I still remember it. We walked under the forest. There was just a small path. We had to climb over the tree trunks without shoes, just sandals.

In the Central Park, next to the Palace [in Guatemala City], there was a map with a sign that said, "This land is for the Todos Santeros." Even before my papa went, other family members had gone to see it. No one lived there. On this side of the river, fishermen came, but on the other side, there was no one.

The Todos Santeros arrived and looked for a place to build a hamáca. Using the hamáca, they began to work. My papa, my uncles, and other friends planted milpa. They were all Todos Santeros. None of them exist anymore except my papa.

Then the *ladinos* [those of Spanish descent with little or no indigenous blood] began to arrive. Because of the work the Todos Santeros had done, they could cross over the river. Finqueros began coming, crossing the hamáca and clearing their pastures. The finqueros said that they were the owners of the land, that it belonged to them and not to the indigenous. In time, they fenced in the land, little by little pushing the people to one side. They cleared pasture and ran cattle. How could one live among the cattle? People had to move their houses. They were all sent off the land. And so the people returned to Todos Santos.

Rosa Jiménez García

Meanwhile, the project of the Ixcán Co-operative had begun. My father came down for a second time with Padre Eduardo Doheney. It was in 1965 if I'm not mistaken. We were the first to arrive. There was not even a path. No one had passed through there. "Papa," we asked, "why did you bring us here when you had land with our grandparents there in Todos Santos? Why?"

Papa bought his parcela in Ixcán, and we went to live there. I remember we lived with my parents on the parcela for two years. Then I came to work for Doña Mima (Mirna Hollstegge). I didn't receive even one class in school. I studied first with Doña Aimée (Hollstegge). Then I began taking evening classes in Mayalan. The teachers were from Ixtuacán. They taught me a little. I learned to read and write. Here in San Juan, I finished second grade. I stopped there.

In Ixcán, we laughed so much. We played, went swimming without any clothes, in the style of Adam and Eve. With my brothers, we had a good time. We lived happily. Since we were children, we followed behind my mama and papa. The life of children there was happy. My parents went to work. One time, they brought home a wild pig. The pigs would come around by the hundreds. They traveled together in packs. My parents were able to kill one, and we ate the meat. Good meat . . . . One remembers . . . . If there is a lot for the pigs to eat, they don't come into the corn fields. They eat plants and live on the riverbanks. There is something like bananas that is their main food. When we passed and saw that they had been eating, we were afraid. They had recently come by and eaten all those plants but not the milpa. They do eat it, but it is by chance. They look for rivers where there is water. They travel by the hundreds. The solitary ones see someone and leave, running. Those that are in packs will attack you. They kill. If a dog gets in with them, they terminate it. They are dangerous.

I last saw my parents in 1982. I went to Ixcán in December for my vacation. In January, I left there for the last time. I said, "I won't return. If the soldiers kill you, I will also die. I don't want to be left alone."

The army was dropping bombs. Things were serious. Many helicopters flew over in those days. The soldiers surrounded the trails and grabbed the women who were washing at the rivers. It was painful. They raped, they kidnapped. It made me afraid.

As I said, the soldiers came at night. Once, they came to my papa's house. He had not yet arrived. We were sleeping. They woke everyone. They didn't knock, just broke down the door. They shined lights in our faces. Who knows what they wanted? We were trembling ... wondering if they would take us out and kill us. They went into the kitchen and ate all the oranges and fruits that were there, everything we had. In the morning, only the peels were left. "Don't harm us," my papa said. "Eat the fruit but don't harm us." They left to take people from another place and kill them.

On a Sunday, they killed a man. He was tied up and without a head, there on the edge of the path. That is how it was at that time. So I came here to San Juan, Sacatepecez.

One day I heard that my parents had gone. They left on foot. There were no vehicles, nothing. Helicopters were dropping bombs. It was like a firestorm falling on the people of Ixcán. My mother says they didn't want to leave, but they fled into the jungle. There were bombs falling like the rain. So they took to the trail and left. God protected them while they walked to the border. The army arrived in columns, but nothing happened to my parents.

They went through the jungle with my brothers. My sister gave birth on the trail. My niece was born there. My brother-in-law, her husband, carried her and the baby on a wooden chair on his back. She covered the baby. She gave birth and continued on, her clothes wet, my brother-in-law carrying her. They finally arrived in Mexico. There they buried the umbilical cord. They saved themselves in Mexico, not in Guatemala. There was fire in Ixcán. Now, they live in the United States.

In Todos Santos, the army came to burn the house of my cousin, Roberto Jiménez. People saw the army take Roberto in the direction of San Juan, near La Mesilla. They made him walk like he was their horse, carrying their things, their water jugs. They had him tied with two lassos around his neck, pulling him this way and that. If he fell, they dragged him. There, the army killed him. His body appeared in a river near that pueblo.

His brother Joaquín became a guerrilla. When he disappeared, they lived in Ixcán in Centro Cuatro. He worked there in the fields. When he didn't return, the word went out that the river had taken him. The people from the co-operatives got together to look for him but found nothing. Eventually, he was forgotten.

After some time had passed, he appeared. He knew they were going to catch him, so better if he went and turned himself in. He appeared on TV, on Channel 3, with the president. There was a lot of commotion, Joaquín Jiménez, a head of ORPA, the guerrillas . . . ."I am a member of the ORPA. I disappeared, yes, but I really went into the guerrillas so the government would do something for the people. The people deserve better. The rich take what they want." He was bringing to light all that was going on. He turned himself in because of fear.

Teresa de Jesús Rafael Cordona
Cuarto Pueblo, February 12, 2011

I was born on the ninth of March 1959, in Santiago Petatan, municipality of Concepción Huista, Huehuetenango. I was ten years old when my father participated in a meeting at the church in Concepción. They said that there was a priest who was going to look for land in Ixcán for the campesinos who didn't have land of their own. And so my papa began the process.

We joined with a group of neighbors who came down to Mayalan, walking from our pueblo. In three days, we arrived at the road crossing to get to Barillas. From there, we walked to San Ramón in one day; on the second day, we got to Mayalan. My father brought us in the year 1974, in the month of December.

When we came down to Mayalan, we were able to rent land with the neighbors to plant something in anticipation of what we would need. The idea was to come and live there, but since we were a family, we first came to plant. We only stayed one month and then returned to our pueblo.

When we went down again, they sent us directly to Pueblo Nuevo, Tercer Pueblo. I was fifteen years old when we first came. We looked for sponsors to monitor us. They were to watch and see what kind of attitude each associate had, to see if they were responsible.

At that time, the people were clearing the center of Pueblo Nuevo. There were lots of trees burning in the jungle. They began to clear a path to Cuarto Pueblo. For two days, the men were opening paths. They made shelters in the jungle, bringing food for two days. Then they began to open a clearing to build a runway.

We were like a party in a galera on the bank of a river. We had been there for two years, working with a sponsor in Cuarto Pueblo, when they distributed parcelas. Little by little, we moved here to Cuarto Pueblo. The co-operative was very beautiful then. We never thought of going to another place. Here we cultivated everything we ate, yucca, sweet potatoes, everything. We didn't need much money. We bartered with the others in the co-operative.

When I was seventeen, someone began to ask my father for me in marriage. Because my papa liked to give us small jobs in the fields, my idea was to get married at twenty-five. When the family came to ask for me, I told them to wait for me three years, to see if they would persevere. But they said they'd wait a year and a half, no more.

On the day of the marriage, all my family went on foot from Cuarto to Pueblo Nuevo to celebrate the wedding. They prepared a big fiesta. While we were waiting, we received the news that Padre Guillermo's plane had been brought down. And so I returned to my house for another three months.

In March, when a new priest arrived, I was married. Now when the people remember the anniversary of the padre's death, I think of my life. Now one can decide if they are going to marry. Before, women were obliged to marry. At that time, if I wanted a parcela, I had to marry first. And so in order to have land, I married a bit quickly. My plan was to stay longer with my father, but there was an opportunity to receive a parcela. Thanks to that, I have land for my children.

I had lived with my late husband for four years when the army massacred him. In an assembly, people had elected him to work in the co-operative. There were nine at a meeting in the co-operative building when the army came to kill, or I should say to kidnap them, because we never found his body.

The next day, together with a friend, I went to see the soldiers. We saw a cadaver with olive green on top, but underneath were civilian clothes. They had a lasso here, another there. It smelled bad, the bodies of the dead. We watched as they began putting them in

Teresa de Jesús Rafael Cordona

a hole. Then they burned them with gasoline. The soldiers said to us, "It wasn't us who killed your husband; it was the guerrillas. They killed him. Don't be afraid of us. We will give you food, housing." But we didn't believe them. "You were lucky," they said, "that you came at this time. If you had come earlier, you would not have returned to your house, because we killed the teacher who was with a student." They'd been guarding their fort when the student came over a hill with a teacher. They fired and killed them. That, they admitted, was done by them.

That was a bit difficult for us. I didn't know how to speak Spanish. I didn't understand when they spoke. I was very closed in at the house; I didn't go out. Only men participated in the meetings. When we got back after the return, we tried to open the hole, but we didn't succeed.

Because of the fear, we went into the jungle. We were there one year. Eleven months after this, the bigger massacre happened, on the fourteenth of March 1982. We were living in the parcela when it occurred. The night before, I'd dreamed that I was running through a rainstorm. I dreamed that my late father had joined the guerrillas. At nine in the morning, when I began to recount my dream, the shooting started. The army came, throwing bombs. I ran into the jungle carrying my oldest child. My sister carried the smaller one. With the shooting overhead, we fled into the jungle. I had almost gone into town. If I had, I wouldn't be alive now. The majority of the parcelistas suffered. There was much hunger. But saddest of all, so many died, and only the children were left.

When we got to Mexico, they told me I would be a representative for the widows. They took me to Mérida. I didn't know how to talk to people from Holland or from other European countries. When they asked me what the women needed, I could only say three words, the three words that were all I knew in Spanish. Eventually, we formed the organization that you knew about, Mama Maquín. I began to go out into other departments, and I have gone to other countries for the work. We organized bee-raising projects with the widows and elders.

We participated in the return. Many of us were women. The CP [Permanent Commission] was made up of men and women. That helped us to learn the process of negotiating the return to Guatemala.

After the return, when we'd been in Victoria for one year, we united again. The helicopters flew over in the night to give food to the army. But our organization was very strong. We demonstrated at the places where there were soldiers, demanding their withdrawal.

As the people were arriving here in Cuarto Pueblo, one of my sons said there was smoke. When the army left, they burned all their things, leaving this place abandoned.

But there was danger. Two boys had gone by the river to work on their parcela. There was an old ambush site. Someone bumped a bomb's antenna. The two died; one was thirty years old, the other fifteen.

Other explosives were missed by the de-miners. Just above my house, we found a bomb. Many encountered those mines. Now, there is not so much talk of all that. When people build, that is when they encounter them.

I didn't remarry. It is the custom here, if you remarry, in a sense, you abandon your first children. The other children are the ones that inherit. I thought that I had to fight for the blood of my late husband, for the parcela. So, for my children's sake, I didn't remarry. Thanks be to God my children did all right in their lives. No, I didn't remarry. But I do have two more children who were a gift.

The work I have now has made me reflect on everything. The good experiences, the bad ones as well . . . .

I am an adviser for the parish, the coordinator for the women of the church. We work with the grandparents who endured the opening up of Ixcán. They are bedridden. We organize visits, prayers, or do something for them, give something to them. Because they are the ones who suffered coming to this place. We value that they are still alive.

We teach the women about the situation we live in. The times we're living today are different from the way things were before.

There have been a lot of changes. When we returned, the young people were much different from before. Many can speak Spanish.

They do what they want. They go to Cancún. Now their way of speaking is complicated. Their way of living . . . .

Before we left, the young men, everyone, worked in the parcela. This generation is not the same. Now they might work, or not . . . . However in their studies, they go further than before. The majority of girls finish sixth grade, middle school. Before, this didn't happen. There is positive and negative in the life we have now.

The work in the churches is also better, Protestant and Catholic. There are education programs; there is youth participation. We have a group that will meet today about migrants, those who are in the United States and in Mexico. There are many, more than one or two hundred. We are just a small group, trying to deal with the problem. There are possibilities. We just received a seed grant to begin, in the amount of twenty-one thousand quetzales. With this money, we must do well . . . . If not, the parish will take it back and give it to others who need it. The grant is for organizing those who have sons in the United States. The migrants, when they're in the States, suffer a lot. For whatever problem, there is a parish, a coordinator who should have information to help them.

An example: If my son was arrested, how would I know? I wouldn't. But I can now go to the parish and begin to search for names, and other information.

In Cancún, there is a house for the migrants who are on the street. The local diocese organized that. They are setting up a communication network for migrants. Also in the States, if there is any problem, we want to know. I can find out how my son is. If he has some problem, I can find out. Before, if a son was arrested, one couldn't ask, one couldn't communicate, but now, someone can start investigating.

Last year, we struggled hard against alcoholism, trying to understand where the problem comes from. We got together and met with the authorities. Now, we have regulations. We are beginning to put things in order. This year, a woman became the mayor of Cuarto Pueblo. She is a catechist from the church. There are two of us, three with her, who are working with the alcoholism problem.

But in the future, what will happen? Will more women enter public office or not? That is our concern.

I remember the bad things; that is lamentable. If I had died . . . . Perhaps there is nothing after death. But I console myself. What would have happened if I'd died and my children were left alone.

Nicolás Rafael Cordona
Andrea Cordona Gregorio
Santiago López Hernández
Cuarto Pueblo, February 12, 2011

Nicolás:
My town of origin is Santiago Petaten, Concepción Huista, Huehuetenango. I speak the Popti, or Jacalteco, dialect. I arrived in Ixcán in April 1975. In Huehue, we had to wait a week for a flight, and came to Pueblo Nuevo in a small plane with my family. Other families had to walk, but we were lucky, we came with a flight. I think it was you, Miguel, who was flying the plane. We spent the rest of 1975 in Pueblo Nuevo. In February of 1976, we had to move here to Cuarto Pueblo.

We opened the path from Pueblo Nuevo to Cuarto Pueblo, and began working on the airstrip. Everyone who was coming from Pueblo Nuevo and those who had stopped in Mayalan or Xalbal but received their parcela in Cuarto Pueblo, all worked on the airstrip. You and I have known each other since our arrival in Ixcán. One time, there was a drunk in the plane, and you took him off. "I don't want a drunk aboard," you said. I still remember that.

We had been here seven years when the violence started. In 1981, when I was the auxiliary mayor here in Cuarto Pueblo, there was a battle between the guerrillas and the army. Seventeen or eighteen co-op directors died in that confrontation. They were here in the center when the attack began. They were taken to the fort. There they were killed. My sister and her husband died. I went to see. We saw the bodies but couldn't identify them. That is how the year 1981 ended.

1982 began . . . January, February . . . On the fourteenth of March was the big massacre here in Cuarto Pueblo. I was on my parcela. My children and my mother and father were here in the center. My mother escaped, but my father remained. She escaped, running. My children got out. They also ran. Thanks be to God, they are here with me. They now have their own families.

Andrea:

I ran from the shooting. They were killing the people. My husband was in the market. People couldn't get out. He was killed by the army. I ran to the parcela. It was one and a half leagues away. I was sick with grief because my husband had remained behind.

Santiago:

All the people were thin and weak. They couldn't withstand it. Many died here in the jungle. We weren't able to continue on here, but we were able to take Andrea to Puerto Rico. When she was sick, she couldn't walk. We carried her. It is close to here, but it took two days through the jungle. We took her out so she wouldn't die here. Her son took her to Comitan so the doctors could cure her.

Nicolás:

She suffered. We had to carry her, moving from place to place when the army came near. Finally, we couldn't do anything, and so Santiago and other compatriots took her to Mexico. When they arrived in Puerto Rico, Mexico, there was an airstrip and aid from the Mexican government.

After that date, we fled into the jungle. Others went to Mexico. I stayed another year and a half here in the jungle because I had my animals, my house. But the repression got worse, and we had to go to Mexico

In the year 1983, I was with my family and others in Mexico, in Puerto Rico, on the border. The Catholic Church and the Mexican government sent us some aid to live on. Later, as the violence worsened, the Guatemalan army crossed over the border, searching for us. My family and I had to go to Quintana Roo. We were there for ten years.

Nicolás Rafael Cordona

Andrea Cordona Gregorio

I was part of the negotiations by the Permanent Committee of Representatives of the Refugees in Mexico. I participated in the negotiations for five years until we reached an accord on the conditions for a return to Guatemala. On the eighth of October of 1992, we signed the agreement. In 1993, we came with the first return.

Miguel, you saw how we came back from Mexico, how many days it took to get to the border. It took more than a month to get to Ixcán, to Victoria 20th of January. That is where we, the first returnees, were concentrated. The name Victoria 20th of January came from the date we crossed the border at La Mesilla.

We arrived in groups from the end of January through February when the last groups arrived in Victoria.

When we were still in Mexico, we appointed a commission to come and construct large shelters in Victoria. They were helped by the neighbors there, who are from Santa Clara. So when we arrived, shelters were already prepared.

Those of us who were from the co-operatives, the associates of the co-operatives Mayalan, Pueblo Nuevo, Los Angeles, of Xalbal, were in Victoria for one year, planning how we would move back to each co-operative. Thanks to the help of the Permanent Commissions and the national and international organizations, we were able to return to our own co-operatives.

The first families arrived here in Cuarto Pueblo the twentieth of April. That's why we celebrate the twentieth of April each year. There was danger from the many bombs, many explosives. It was a problem. But through the United Nations, ACNUR, the bomb detectors came. They began to search for bombs in the area. I don't know how many years they were here, but even after they left, more bombs appeared. We would call the police and the army, and they came to detonate them.

We built a large school. We ourselves had to bring the building materials on our backs from Victoria. Over the whole time, we carried more than twenty *quintales* [two thousand pounds] per person. Walking to Victoria is two hours normally, but with cargo, three or four hours. It's more than eleven kilometers (just over six and a half

Santiago López Hernández

miles). In that way, we continued construction of the community buildings, the health center, the churches. The churches were first built with logs, boards, and roofing tin. We began to build our houses of wood.

Then there was no road, just an open cut through the jungle. That is how all the families came back. We began to solicit for a road from Victoria to the river, and from the river to Cuarto Pueblo, and from Cuarto to Pueblo Nuevo. It was difficult, but we now have a road. It's not a good one, but at least we can travel.

What a story, Miguel. This is not something made up. It is something we have lived with our own flesh and blood. You and I didn't see each other for years. We didn't know how the other was. But thanks be to God, we are still alive.

Glossary of Spanish Words and Abbreviations

ACNUR *Alto Comisionado de las Naciones Unidas para los Refugiados.* The United Nations High Commission for Refugees.

Aldea Hamlet. Maybe three or four houses, maybe a dozen or more.

Atole A drink made from corn flour.

B-8 A survey coordinate that became the name of the center located there.

Bodega A warehouse. The one in Mayalan was a large thatch-covered space where boards were stored for building the clinic, store, etc.

Brechas Openings cut through the jungle for a path, survey line, or road.

Campesino A farmer—in the Ixcan usually, but not always, indigenous.

Catequista Catechist.

Chamaca Mexican colloquialism for a little girl.

COMAR *Comisión Mexicana de Ayuda a Refugiados*, Mexican Commission for the Aid of Refugees.

Compañera Feminine of compañero. Also used as girlfriend and, at times, wife.

Compañero Person working with another with a common aim.

CONALFA *Comite Nacional de Alfabetización,* National Committee for the Teaching of Reading and Writing.

Coyote The animal, but also a person who smuggles others across the border.

CPR *Comunidades de Poblacion en Resistencia,* Communities of the People in Resistance. The civilian communities that survived in the jungle, hiding from the army, for fourteen to sixteen years.

Cuerda Common measure of land in the Ixcán. Most farms were four hundred cuerdas, or twenty-eight acres.

EGP *Ejército Guerrillero de los Pobres,* Guerrilla Army of the Poor.

Finca Plantation, ranch, or large farm.

Finquero The owner of a finca.

FRG *Frente Republicano Guatemalteco,* Guatemalan Republican Front, a right-wing political party now known as the Institutional Republican Party.

Galera A large shelter made with posts and a thatch roof.

Hamaca Literally a hammock but also describing a suspension bridge, some small enough that people must cross single file, others big enough for mules to cross.

INTA *Instituto Nacional de Transformacion Agraria,* the National Institute of Agrarian Reform.

Ixcán At the time referred to in this book, the land between the Rio Ixcán and Rio Xalbal, from the Mexican border south to an east-west line generally about eight to ten miles south of Mexico.

Mam One of the indigenous peoples of Guatemala.

Mano de Obra Labor in general, also the obligatory labor done by campesinos for the government, such as road building. In the co-operatives, it was work that was done for the community, like building an airstrip.

Marimbistas Marimba players, musicians.

Mercado Market.

Milpa Corn and beans planted together.

MINUGUA The United Nations Verification Mission in Guatemala, a U.N. humanitarian agency that involved a three-month peacekeeping mission at the most critical point in the peace process, and also was instrumental in organizing the returns of the refugees.

Mojado Literally "wet." It also is used to imply someone who is in a country illegally. The term comes from those who got "wet" crossing the Rio Grande from Mexico into the United States.

Morrál A shoulder bag.

ONU *Organización de las Naciones Unidas,* the United Nations.

ORPA *Organización Revolucionario del Pueblo en Armas,* Revolutionary Organization of the People in Arms, one of the four groups of armed resistance during the civil war.

Padrino Sponsor, godfather.

Paisano Fellow countryman

Parcela A plot of land, farm, or homestead. The lands given out through the Cooperativa Ixcán Grande were referred to as parcelas.

Parcelista One who owns a parcela, a member of the co-operative.

Patrón Boss, chief, master.

Tierra fría Literally "cold land," the term used to refer to the highlands.

Tigre A jaguar. There is also the "tigrillo," an ocelot.

Tumbál A conga drum, carried with a strap around the musician's shoulders.

URNG *Unidad Revolucionaria Nacional Guatemalteca,* Guatemalan National Revolutionary Unity, a political party that started as a guerrilla movement but laid down its arms in 1996.

Violón Double bass.

About the Author

Born and raised in northwestern Illinois, Michael Sullivan studied aeronautical engineering at the University of Colorado following a tour of duty in Vietnam. In 1972, he got a pilot's license and traveled south, meeting Father Bill Woods in Guatemala, flying for the land reform project that was reshaping the Ixcan region, and meeting the people he later interviewed for this book.

Sometimes it's said in the foreign service that one's first overseas posting is the one that stays in the heart. For Sullivan, that has been true of the Ixcan; he's been back time and time again. Though he has been called a pilot-anthropologist, he says instead that, "I was simply a good listener, interacting with the people of Ixcan who had become trusted friends over a period of forty years."

Early in his flying days, he sought to become an airline pilot, and asked a friend working in the industry for a reference. The friend refused, saying he saw someone who would be driven crazy by the monotony of flying the same route over and over. Instead, Sullivan embraced his love of adventure and began exploring the world. He drove a small Honda motorcycle down to Guatemala, where he first began work as a bush pilot.

He has since taken his love of flying around the world, working throughout Central America, Alaska, Indonesia, and Africa—including many years with Jacques-Yves Cousteau and the Cousteau Society.

He and his equally adventurous—and eternally patient—wife, Tina, have passed on their love of adventure and appreciation of different cultures to their five children. His work as a pilot, in addition to being something he loves, has also enabled him to bring positive change to the world as a humanitarian and environmentalist. He has quietly worked as a documentary photographer, videographer, and photojournalist throughout his life to protect and support the communities and environment of the places he's come to love.

He is the author, with photojournalist Tony O'Brien, of *Afghan Dreams*, a book of haunting images and interviews with Afghan children talking about their lives, fears, and dreams.

Sullivan lives now in Santa Fe, New Mexico.